'Having researched and written on the theology of death and dying for well over thirty years, Paul Badham has long ago proved himself a leader in the field. Few can speak with such authority. You may not like what he says but the evidence he adduces to argue the case for assisted dying and the biblical and theological arguments he marshals will persuade you of the importance of making up your mind on this issue before personal circumstances or legal developments force you to decide in a hurry. I have greatly enjoyed reading this book and highly recommend it.'

The Revd Dr Peter C. Jupp, Department of Theology and Religion,
University of Durham, founding co-editor of Mortality

'Though Christian leaders are on the whole opposed to any relaxation of the law against "Mercy Killing", they seldom explicitly base their arguments on Christian doctrine or the New Testament. Professor Badham's book is extremely valuable because it examines the controversy in the light of the specifically Christian virtues of faith, hope and compassion, and comes down on the side of carefully controlled assisted dying for the terminally ill. Both believers and non-believers will benefit greatly from this consistently reasonable and compassionate account of the euthanasia debate.'

Mary Warnock, philosopher

'Although I do not agree with Professor Badham's conclusion, I respect the clarity and care with which he marshals his arguments. His book is a serious and important contribution to a serious and important debate.'

The Revd Dr John Polkinghorne, KBE, FRS

'Very timely, very accessible, this book will bring much relief to thousands of Christians who support the case for assisted dying, yet wrongly think the Christian faith cannot endorse it. Badham gently but convincingly makes his case, attending to the scriptures, the Christian hope and the arguments of opponents. The book is a triumph for liberal, relevant, compassionate, readable theology.'

A... ... *Applied Theology,*
...ity of Exeter

D0494414

'Most people, including many regular churchgoers, support the legalization of voluntary euthanasia. However most theologians (including myself) do not. Given this sharp contrast, Professor Badham has long been a rare and vital exception. His compassionate and accessible Christian voice does need to be heard. I welcome this book and commend others to buy it and then to read it carefully.'

Robin Gill, Michael Ramsey Professor of Modern Theology
at the University of Kent

'This book is written with integrity and compassion. Paul Badham addresses the sensitive issues surrounding assisted dying from an essentially Christian perspective that takes seriously the deeply held views of those who oppose it, but offers an argument based on theological understanding and human experience that is very persuasive. It is a real contribution to the debate.'

The Revd Baroness Richardson of Calow

* * *

Paul Badham has been Professor of Theology and Religious Studies in the University of Wales, Lampeter, since 1991. He is a vice-president of the Modern Churchpeople's Union, a patron of Dignity in Dying and an Anglican priest. Religious and ethical beliefs concerning life, death and immortality have been one of the major areas of his research.

He is the author of *Christian Beliefs about Life after Death* (SPCK, 1978), co-author of *Immortality or Extinction?* (SPCK, 1984), editor of *Religion, State and Society in Modern Britain* (Mellen, 1989), *Ethics on the Frontiers of Human Existence* (Paragon, 1992) and co-editor of *Death and Immortality in the Religions of the World* (Paragon, 1987), *Perspectives on Death and Dying* (The Charles Press, 1989) and *Facing Death* (University of Wales Press, 1996).

His main articles in this area are: 'Should Christians Accept the Validity of Voluntary Euthanasia?', *Studies in Christian Ethics*, October 1995. Reprinted in Robin Gill, *Euthanasia and the Churches* (Cassell, 1998), 'Euthanasia and the Christian Doctrine of God', *Studies in Christian Ethics*, June 1998, and 'The Modern Churchpeople's Union Submission on the Assisted Dying Bill', *Modern Believing*, April 2005.

IS THERE A CHRISTIAN CASE FOR ASSISTED DYING?

Voluntary euthanasia reassessed

PAUL BADHAM

SPCK

*To my father Leslie. This book is, in part,
my attempt to grapple with some of the questions
he faced in his final months of life.*

First published in Great Britain in 2009

Society for Promoting Christian Knowledge
36 Causton Street
London SW1P 4ST

British Library Cataloguing-in-Publication Data
A catalogue record for this book is available from the British Library

ISBN 978–0-281–05919–5

1 3 5 7 9 10 8 6 4 2

Typeset by Graphicraft Ltd, Hong Kong
Printed in Great Britain by Ashford Colour Press

Produced on paper from sustainable forests

Contents

Questioning

What is all this suffering for?
  Asks the dawdler at death's door;
What strange God would make this pain
  Come again and come again,
Wear down life and dull the brain?

Is all our faith and love but loss?
  Ask the sufferer on the Cross.
Is it reason, is it madness, is it chance –
  Those cruel thorns and nails, and lance?
Is it the test of faith perchance?

'Though He slay me, I will trust Him'
  Never shall my faith grown dim.
All the terms of being human (even pain)
  Are the price of sensitivity and our gain
For 'tis the souls that overcome who rise again

To this truth I give my heart
  In which a lifetime's thinking has a part.
We must trust our finest feeling;
  Even when one's brain is reeling
For God's suffering love has meaning.
                    (Leslie Badham, 1975)

The Revd Leslie Badham (1908–75) was Vicar of Windsor and one of her Majesty's Chaplains. He was the author of several books, including *Verdict on Jesus* and *Love Speaks from the Cross*. In 1965 he contracted prostate cancer from which he died ten years later.

Foreword

The issue of assisted dying for terminally ill patients is one that arouses passionate and opposing views. Those in favour seek only to prevent unnecessary suffering. And public-opinion surveys consistently show that in the order of 80 per cent of the population support a change in the law, so as to allow terminally ill and mentally competent adults the option to end their suffering, by ending their lives with the assistance of their doctors.

Those against, who number about 20 per cent of the population, argue that to assist a terminally ill patient to die will put vulnerable people at risk. They sometimes concede that some patients suffer terrible deaths, but believe they should continue suffering rather than run the risk of vulnerable members of society being harmed. To meet such objections, I was anxious to ensure that appropriate safeguards to protect the old and the vulnerable were built into my Assisted Dying for the Terminally Ill Bill, and I had hoped that the parliamentary debate would focus on ensuring that adequate safeguards were indeed in place.

In the course of the controversies aroused by my Bill, however, it became apparent that many of the opponents of assisted dying were not really concerned to explore such safeguards. Their real objections were more fundamental than this and derived from their religious beliefs. Certainly, most of the lobbying against my Bill came from Christian organizations. It is therefore important that this issue should be explored from the perspective of the Christian faith, as this gets to the root of the beliefs that underpin and influence their opposition.

That is why Professor Badham's book is so important. In it, he courageously and incisively explores the historical background to the Churches' negative attitude towards assisted dying. He examines carefully the theological and ethical arguments on both sides, particularly in relation to Christian beliefs about the nature of faith, hope and love. Above all, he emphasizes the primacy for

Christians of the ethical teaching of Jesus himself. He notes that Jesus' own summary of all religious law was that we should love our neighbour as ourselves, and concludes:

> When peoples' sufferings are so great that they make repeated requests to die, it seems a denial of that loving compassion which is supposed to be the hallmark of Christianity to refuse to allow their requests to be granted. If we truly love our neighbours as ourselves how can we deny them the death we would wish for ourselves in such a condition?

I myself find it impossible to answer that question and suspect that the opponents of assisted dying will also have no credible answer.

Joel Joffe

Acknowledgements

I am greatly indebted to my former colleague in the Death and Immortality programme at Lampeter, Professor David Cockburn, for suggesting that I should write on Christian ethics in relation to euthanasia for his book on the value of human life. This began the process that has led to this book. I thank Professor Claude Villee of Harvard Medical School for co-chairing with me the Washington Conference on 'Ethics on the Frontiers of Human Existence' where I met so many leading figures in bioethical discussions, including Helga Kuhse, Patrick Nowell Smith and Robert Winston. I thank Professor Robin Gill as President of the British Society for the Study of Christian Ethics for his invitation to me to address their annual conference on the question 'Should Christians Accept the Validity of Voluntary Euthanasia?' and for including that lecture and responses to it in his book *Euthanasia and the Churches*. I thank Professor Linda Woodhead for including me in the special volume of *Studies in Christian Ethics* devoted to euthanasia. I am most grateful to Professor Paul Ballard for convening the 'Facing Death' Seminar in Cardiff and for my numerous discussions with the members of that seminar and particularly with Baroness Finlay in the seminar's monthly meetings. I thank the Modern Churchpeople's Union for entrusting to me their response to the Assisted Dying Bill, and I thank Lord Joffe for including me in the All Souls' Conference on the responses he received. I thank Dignity in Dying for the great honour they have done me in inviting me to be one of their patrons, and the help that their research staff (particularly Davina Hehir and Carmen Dupont) have given me in locating data. Without all these many contributions over the years this book would not have been written. Finally, I thank Rebecca Mulhearn at SPCK for her help and advice in bringing the book towards its final state.

Acknowledgements

My father's poem 'Questioning' was written during the last weeks of his life. It has not yet been published, but we arranged for it to be printed on the service sheet for his Memorial Service from where I have taken it.

Introduction

An inter-Christian debate

This book is a contribution to the inter-Christian debate on the question of assisted dying. Christian leadership is generally opposed to this, but ordinary churchgoers say they would greatly welcome legalization to permit assistance in dying for people suffering unbearably in the final stages of terminal illness. The book explores the theological issues behind the current debate, and examines the principal moral arguments used by Christians in two influential ethical traditions. It considers the morality of assisted dying in the light of the biblical evidence and of Jesus' own approach to moral questions. The book also considers how this debate reflects the Christian understanding of our relationship with God and the theological value of suffering. One important theme in this book is the relevance of the Christian belief in life after death to the way we should approach our own dying. The book includes an examination and comparison of end-of-life decision-making in Britain, the Netherlands and the US State of Oregon and ends with an attempt to present a Christian case for assisted dying.

Voluntary euthanasia and assisted dying

Throughout this book reference is made to both voluntary euthanasia and to assisted dying. In either case it is axiomatic that this is in the context of a competent person suffering unbearably in terminal illness who explicitly and repeatedly requests assistance to die. In either case adequate safeguards need to be in place to ensure that this is truly the patient's own decision. The difference between the two is that in voluntary euthanasia a doctor will administer medication leading to death, while in assisted dying, though the doctor provides the medication, responsibility for taking it is left to the patient. Euthanasia is legal in the Netherlands and Belgium whereas in Switzerland and Oregon only assisted dying is permitted. In 2008 Luxembourg legalized both possibilities. The legislation proposed by Lord Joffe in 2006 followed the example of Oregon in seeking the legalization of assisted dying. I shall discuss Lord Joffe's Bill in Chapter 5. Essentially it was a bill concerned solely with mentally 'competent' people, who were suffering unbearably in the final stages of terminal illness and who repeatedly asked for assistance to die. Two doctors had to confirm that realistically nothing further could be done to restore them to health and that they would almost certainly die within weeks and at the most within six months. A solicitor had to witness the written request and a variety of further safeguards was built into the bill, as we shall see later. The bill was discussed at length by a committee of the House of Lords that collected a vast range of evidence from interested parties. Ultimately the bill was defeated, at least in part, by a very well-orchestrated campaign against it by a range of Christian organizations, and by the unanimous opposition of the Bench of Bishops in the House of Lords.

Dignity in Dying, a leading campaigning organization promoting patient choice at the end of life, supported all the safeguards in Lord Joffe's Bill. However, it is possible that in supporting a future bill they may wish to extend assistance to that very small number of mentally 'competent' people who are no longer able to self-administer. Voluntary euthanasia is the term most widely used in the literature and so, except when it is vital to discriminate, that is the expression most often used in this book.

Moral issues concerned with switching off life-support systems

Because the book is focused on voluntary euthanasia/assisted dying there is no sustained discussion of the morality of withdrawing or withholding life-support systems because it is now accepted that these are issues of clinical judgement rather than of morality. The guidance of the British Medical Association is that

2

Why euthanasia and assisted dying have become major issues of concern

During the past 40 years there has been a strong shift in public opinion in favour of permitting voluntary euthanasia in cases of unbearable suffering in terminal illness. In 1969 only 51 per cent of the British population supported voluntary euthanasia. By 1985 72 per cent declared themselves in favour and by 2006 that figure had risen to at least 82 per cent.[1] Comparable changes in public opinion have taken place in the USA, Canada, Australia and Europe. In the Netherlands and Belgium, voluntary euthanasia is now permitted, and in the State of Oregon physician-assisted suicide has been legalized. In 2008 Luxembourg legalized both possibilities. In Switzerland it has never been a crime to assist another person to commit suicide, provided one in no way benefited from that person's death. In recent years this provision in Swiss law has been used by the society Dignitas to enable people from other countries to travel to Switzerland to take advantage of this provision.

I suggest that there are two reasons why voluntary euthanasia has gained popular support and become a major ethical issue. The first is that modern housing, sanitation, central heating, technology and medicine have united to enable us to stave off death for far longer than was ever possible in the past. This has created a situation where some people are enabled to live on into a situation where they would actually prefer to die, rather than have any further extension of their earthly existence. The second reason is that we have gradually become increasingly autonomous: we have become used to deciding for ourselves what we do with our lives, and many feel that this freedom of choice should also extend to choosing the moment at which to abandon the struggle against terminal illness and to seek assistance to die.

On reaching our full span of life

One of the most striking features of the past hundred and fifty years has been a steady rise in the average age of death. No longer do half of us die before the age of five. No longer is giving birth profoundly life-threatening to women, and no longer will most of us succumb to infectious disease in mid-life. The majority of us can now look forward to a 'third age' in life after we have finished with work, when we can enjoy a life of leisure. However, there has actually been virtually no change in what one might call the natural human span of life.

The classic description of the human lifespan appears in Psalm 90.10 (Book of Common Prayer):

> The days of our age are threescore years and ten;
> and though men be so strong that they come to fourscore years:
> yet is their strength then but labour and sorrow;
> so soon passeth it away, and we are gone.

What this tells us is that, for the last three thousand years or so, it has been the human experience that, if we do not succumb earlier to accident or disease we can usually expect to live to our seventies, and the stronger among us can live into our eighties. But after we get into our eighties life is very much a struggle. This remains the human condition for the vast majority of us. Even though there have always been people who have lived on into their nineties and hundreds, it remains the case that, for most elderly people, their eighties prove to be a fatal decade. The most significant difference between today and the situation in former ages is not the existence of old age, but that the majority of us in the developed world can reasonably expect to live to see it.

Why more of us live longer

Sanitation, central heating, better nutrition and availability of antibiotics are key factors here. Elderly people no longer have to venture out of their homes in all weathers to visit a chemical toilet at the end of their gardens – the *Ty Bach* or 'little house' as it used to be referred to in Welsh. They also no longer have to struggle outside to a coal-shed, to carry in scuttles full of coal to fuel a fire around which they try to huddle for warmth during the winter months. In the past every winter was a challenge to the aged. Central heating and double glazing have arguably done more than anything else to add years to our lives. It is also the case that the ready availability, and ease of preparation, of nutritious food makes it far easier than in the past to ensure adequate nourishment. Medicine too has played an important role, with vaccination and antibiotics shielding us from the ravages of infectious diseases that in the past proved fatal to so many.

It is these factors that caused average human life expectancy to jump from 30 to 67 years during the nineteenth and twentieth centuries. In sixteenth-century London only 5 per cent lived on in their seventies whereas by 1998 75 per cent did so.[2] However, over and above these factors, which have been responsible for the huge rise in life expectancy throughout the world, enhanced medical care now enables us to live on for a few further years in conditions of frailty under which life would have been impossible in past ages.

One development is the provision of oxygen to those with breathing difficulties. Linked by a kind of umbilical cord to their oxygen generator, aged sufferers from respiratory illnesses can enjoy a year or more of additional life in their own homes, while motorized scooters can enable them to venture out long after walking has become impossible. Likewise pills to prevent water retention, pills to lower blood cholesterol, and pills to reduce blood pressure can all help in the fight against heart disease. New cancer treatments can sometimes cure and will frequently enable people to live with the disease for several years beyond when it would have killed them in the past. Pneumonia, formerly known as 'the old man's friend', will no longer release him from this life, for it can readily be treated by antibiotics as can many other formerly fatal infections. In hospitals of course death can be kept further at bay by saline drips and respirators, not to mention kidney dialysis, organ transplants and heart bypass operations. If a person's heart stops beating in an intensive therapy unit, every possible effort at resuscitation will be instantly made, and it is not unknown for this process to be repeated many times before death becomes impossible to resist any longer. In general a host of new technologies and a cornucopia of new drugs can nowadays keep life in being long beyond anything possible in the past.

The new situation created by modern medicine

This has created a new moral situation. As Hans Küng points out, 'for the first time in human history . . . human beings have succeeded, by improving living conditions and by extraordinary progress in medicine . . . in delaying death . . . in some cases by many years'. In the past, death usually came quickly 'in hours, days or at most months'. But now life can be extended with years of old age being followed by a final phase of years of terminal illness.[3]

According to Guy Brown the average person in the West today can expect to die 'from a long drawn out degenerative disease' and may often experience 'ten years of chronic disease and disability before death, and this figure is rising'.[4] Much publicity has been given to the steady increase in life expectancy. Less attention has focused on the fact that a high proportion of the extra time will be spent in terminal illness. Brown notes that between 1991 and 2001 life expectancy in the UK rose by 2.2 years. But years of healthy life only increased by 0.6 years while years of ill health increased by 1.6 years. What is even more disturbing is that 'expected years of ill health are currently rising by one year per decade in the UK while years of health have more or less stopped increasing'.[5]

Richard Nicholson, writing as editor of the *Bulletin of Medical Ethics*, is deeply concerned that there is 'no clear evidence' that much of the funding spent on the health service improves the quality of human life. What he thinks is happening is that

> Health services increase life expectancy by keeping alive people with serious diseases who would otherwise die. Studies on both sides of the Atlantic have found that about half an individual's lifetime

healthcare expenditure occurs in the last six months of life – in other words, a major NHS activity is the prolongation of dying.[6]

Mary Warnock and Elisabeth Macdonald draw attention to the fact that in 2006 the British Government Actuary Department published their calculation that in seventy years' time there will be 1.2 million Britons aged 100 or over and many thousands of 110 or more.[7] This is actually a frightening statistic, given that, the older we live to be, the less likely we are to be healthy or independent. Brown notes that, in 1969, 30 per cent of people in their last year of life needed help in dressing, undressing or washing. This figure had risen to 52 per cent by 1987. In 1972, 20 per cent of the UK population were suffering from chronic illness. By 1998 this figure had risen to 34 per cent.[8]

Life in 'care homes'

Already the majority of very old people spend their final years in hospitals or 'care homes'. In April 2008, the magazine of the Consumers' Association, *Which?*, compared the various financial arrangements available to us to cover the cost of the four years we can expect to live in a care home after spouse or children can no longer cope with caring for us in our own homes. The best plan appears to be to sell our own homes and to use the proceeds to buy an 'immediate need annuity' that will increase by 5 per cent per annum to cover the steady rise in the cost of our twenty-four-hour care.[9] One advantage of this is that the money from the immediate need annuity is tax-free if paid direct to the care home. Saga gives the same advice suggesting that for many people this is the only way to cover the £112,312 cost of a typical four-year stay.[10] Similar advice is given in *The Times*.[11]

Warnock and Macdonald suggest we need to ask 'what all the extra years are actually worth to the people who live them? . . . This question is at its most insistent when old people have reached a condition where their consciousness is totally absorbed by pain and distress and when they have lapsed into dementia.'[12] Dan and Lavinia Cohn-Sherbok, in their 'practical guide to caring for the elderly', give much sensible advice about the difficulties of choosing a good care home, as well as describing in illuminating detail the many infirmities that one can be expected to suffer from in extreme old age.[13] Dr Guy Brown, who heads a research group at Cambridge University on cell death in the brain, the heart and in cancer, sums up the findings published in the journal *Age and Ageing* for 1998 of the symptoms suffered by the terminally ill:

> Those dying from cancer suffered most: 88% suffering pain, 54% breathlessness, 59% nausea and vomiting, 41% difficulty swallowing, 63% constipation, 41% mental confusion, 28% pressure sores, 40% urinary incontinence, and 32% bowel incontinence. Those dying from heart disease or stroke suffered in general somewhat lower levels of these symptoms but for a longer period before death.[14]

The problem of Alzheimer's

From the perspective of the patient's family, the co-residents in the care home and the nursing and medical staff, the most difficult challenge of ageing is the growth in the number of patients suffering from Alzheimer's. This was formerly bracketed with other diseases under the heading 'senile dementia'. This was done with good cause since Alzheimer's is primarily a disease of old age. According to Brown, 'prevalence of the disease is about 1 per cent at 65 years of age and doubles every five years thereafter, so that about 25 per cent of 85-year-olds are thought to have Alzheimer's'. To these we should add those suffering from Alzheimer's precursor, Mild Cognitive Impairment (MCI). Symptoms of MCI include memory loss, not recognizing family and friends and noticeable intellectual decline. This disease affects some 1 per cent of 60-year-olds, rising to 42 per cent of 85-year-olds, so roughly two-thirds of people in their mid eighties will be suffering from MCI or full-blown Alzheimer's.[15]

This is one of the reasons why care homes find it so difficult to recruit adequate staff and why geriatric medicine is so unpopular as a career choice for young doctors. Writing in the *Journal of the Royal Society of Medicine* Dr David Oliver laments the habit of doctors referring to geriatric medicine as 'Market Gardening' (i.e. caring for old patients who they think of as 'cabbages'), or referring to patients as 'crumblies' or 'bed-blockers'. He argues that older people deserve better than this, and that geriatric medicine needs to be given far higher priority in that 70 per cent of hospital beds are occupied by the over-65s, and that by 2025 the percentage of those over 80 years old who are dependent on others for two or more activities of daily living will increase by 50 per cent.[16]

Why these factors lead to the contemplation of euthanasia

For an increasing number of people the Promethean prolongation of life under these circumstances can become so burdensome that they long to be released from it. Even before these new developments Shakespeare had recognized 'the *calamity* of so long life'[17] as being among the greatest of human evils. From a biblical perspective the new medical developments greatly strengthen the judgement of Ecclesiasticus that 'Death is better than a miserable life, and eternal rest than chronic sickness' (Ecclus. 30.17).

One problem with some of the medical procedures now available is that they are frequently employed when there is no longer any realistic hope that the patient will make a recovery from illness and return to independent life. As such these procedures essentially serve simply to prolong the dying process. This is a key factor in the pressure for voluntary euthanasia to be legalized. According to Patrick Nowell Smith, a former president of the World Federation of Right to Die Societies: 'The vast majority of people who join voluntary euthanasia societies are people in their 60s or 70s who are still enjoying life but do not like what they see ahead of them in a society in which more than three-quarters of us will die in institutions.' He describes, as a typical new member of a euthanasia society, a person who saw 'both his father and mother, years apart, suffering helplessly for months when they might have been quietly released'. According to Nowell Smith most supporters of voluntary euthanasia 'dread a similar fate unless the law is changed so that one can choose, if still able, to slip away in dignity from the inhumane methods many hospitals employ today to keep one from dying a natural death'.[18]

According to the research of Clive Seale, 28 per cent of people who have watched a loved one die believe that it would have been better if they had died earlier than they actually did. When asked if their loved one had expressed a wish to die 24 per cent said 'yes'. Of these 36 per cent had explicitly asked for medical help to die.[19]

What people dread in this new situation is not primarily pain or suffering but what Küng describes as the plight of 'being imprisoned in a highly technological medical system, afraid of total dependence and loss of control over their own selves, drugged until they are dozy and sleepy, no longer thinking, no longer drinking, no longer experiencing anything'.[20] According to Douglas Davies in his book, *A Brief History of Death*, fear of death today is often fear of what Francis Fukuyama calls *Our Posthuman Future* in his book of that name. He describes this in terms of 'the national nursing home scenario' for post-80-year-olds in which people live a lonely life 'deprived of those active commitments and obligations to others that make life worthwhile'.[21]

Although with specialist palliative care, physical pain can be controlled in up to 95 per cent of cases,[22] this level of care is not usually available and 'pain in cancer patients is common and often inadequately managed'.[23] Even when pain is properly controlled this by no means prevents people suffering unbearably during their final illness. Some people find the inescapable limitations and humiliations of terminal illness unbearable and want to be released from them. In some cases what is unbearable is that people who are used to being autonomous find themselves wholly dependent on others for everything. In other cases, what people find unbearable is the prospect of nothing further in life to look forward to. Sometimes what is unbearable is not being able to control one's bodily functions. To be doubly incontinent, frequently sick and constantly fighting for breath is simply not the way some people wish to live out their last days nor to be remembered by their loved ones. It is factors like these that have given rise to pro-euthanasia organizations such as Dignity in Dying.

The value of palliative care

Fortunately there has been a growing acceptance both among doctors and church leaders that there is no need to use extraordinary measures to keep people alive in a burdensome situation. Arthur Clough famously wrote:

> Thou shalt not kill;
> But need'st not strive,
> Officiously to keep alive[24]

Although Clough intended this ironically, it has become widely accepted as sound advice. The philosophy behind palliative care and the whole hospice movement is to accept the inevitability of death, to desist from burdensome and futile medical interventions and to help patients live out their last days with as much comfort and dignity as possible. By carefully balancing drugs, doctors, nurses and medical social workers in hospices can normally eliminate pain, and enable people to live out the last stages of life with as much dignity and support as circumstances permit. For many people this is undoubtedly the right solution for them.

Is there a significant difference between letting a person die and assisting a person to die?

The widespread acceptance of the morality of allowing a person to die opens up the question of whether or not there is any morally significant difference between 'letting a person die' and 'assisting a person to die'. Consider the case where a patient asks for a life-support system to be switched off. The result of acceding to that request will lead directly to the patient's death in the same way as would acceding to the patient's request to be supplied with the medical means to end their own life. In both cases the patient will die, and in both cases the death would be the result of the willingness of the medical staff to accede to the patient's wishes. Unfortunately, however, the manner of their dying may not be equally tranquil. Alastair Campbell cites two cases of people whose respirators were switched off but who then struggled for breath before finally dying. In one case it was six days before death intervened.[25]

The problem of being allowed to die a long-drawn-out death

A far more common situation is where we accept the right of a dying person to decline life-sustaining nourishment. This regularly happens as people come close to death. We allow people to choose to die a slow death by gradual starvation, but we deny them the alternative of a quick and painless death that at least some of them might prefer. Consider the case of a patient with inoperable cancer of the stomach. The patient will ultimately reach a stage where he or she no longer wishes to eat, and this stage is likely to coincide with the stage in the development of the disease when the patient would in any case derive little benefit from eating. At this point there are currently two options. One is to provide adequate pain relief while the patient slowly starves to death. The other is to provide pain relief coupled with artificial nutrition and hydration so that the patient survives until the cancer spreads to other organs. Both scenarios are deeply disturbing. Mary Warnock and Elisabeth Macdonald comment on the first that the 'lengthy process (of starving to death) places intolerable anguish on the family and professional carers. It is very hard to watch a loved one die slowly of starvation and dehydration.'[26] Baroness Murphy, a leading specialist in geriatric medicine, says of the second option of 'artificial nutrition and hydration' that these 'are invasive medical treatments . . . They involve the insertion of a nasogastric tube, which is not pleasant at all . . . The process is uncomfortable and very often distressing.' She has given written instructions that she herself is not to be subjected to such 'burdensome treatments'.[27]

Another issue is that to control the pain it is sometimes necessary to increase the pain-killing provision to a level described as 'terminal sedation'. In other words, the only way to control the pain may be to effectively render the patient unconscious until death finally intervenes to end it all. The question immediately arises: 'why should medical staff deny the patient a third option of a swift and painless release?' If pain control can only be achieved by 'terminal sedation' would it not be better to allow the patient to choose death before unconsciousness intervenes?

What is in the patient's best interest?

Almost all people agree that ideally the ultimate aim should be to do what is in the best interest of the patient. Both the World Medical Assembly and the United States President's Commission for the Study of Ethical Problems in Medicine have concluded that 'passive euthanasia' (i.e. 'letting die') could in some cases be preferable to the use of 'extra-ordinary measures' to keep a person alive. In accordance with such guidance the United States Surgeon General ruled that if a patient cannot obtain any nourishment from eating normally there is no obligation to provide nourishment artificially. Instead the patient should be provided with a bed and food by mouth knowing that it was not going to be nutritious and thus be allowed to die. Patrick Nowell Smith cites the case of an 85-year-old patient who starved to death over a 47-day period. He then asks pointedly, 'Who would seriously want to suggest that it is in the patient's best interest to be dehydrated and starved to death?'[28]

It is good that a consensus has arisen that no one should be forced against their will to undergo extra-ordinary or burdensome treatments which cannot benefit them. It is also entirely right that people should have the right to stop eating when they feel their lives have come to their natural end. Allowing a person to die naturally, however, can mean in practice that they have a harder death than if they were given means to end their lives in a more direct manner. This is why some people who have watched their parents, grandparents or friends undergo a greatly extended dying process would like to be able to choose an alternative way of dying for themselves. That is why the pressure for legalizing voluntary euthanasia has grown because of, rather than in spite of, the magnificent advances made by medical science in recent decades.

The growth of personal autonomy

The other pressure for legalizing euthanasia today is the growing experience of freedom of choice (individual autonomy) in almost every other aspect of life. For most of human history people have had very limited choices. Before the rise of modern transport, horizons were limited by how far people could walk or ride. This meant that most people lived out their entire lives in the small communities in which they grew up. Their choices of what jobs they would do, where they would live, what they would eat, and whom they would marry, were all fairly circumscribed by the conditions pertaining in their village. Until the industrial revolution most people's lives were dominated by the agricultural seasons, and the need to grow the food necessary for survival. The success of the local harvest determined whether they would be well-fed or starve in the following year and most people worked on the land. When illness struck there was very little that could be done to treat it. In this context belief in 'particular providence' seemed entirely natural. In other words most people believed implicitly that God determined everything that happened in life. Naturally we could seek to influence his decisions through our prayers, but in the end we had to accept what God decreed for us.

What has happened in the past 200 years is that this belief pattern has profoundly changed even among deeply committed Christians. Compared with any generation before us we, in the developed world, have almost unlimited choices of how we should live out our lives. We choose what jobs we will do, where we should live, what kind of foods we should eat, where we will spend our holidays, with whom we will socialize, etc. etc. Instead of most of life following a predictable pattern we can choose our own lifestyles. This affects our most basic life experiences. In the past children were seen as inevitable concomitants of a married existence and large families were the inevitable norm. Now contraception enables us to choose whether and when to have children. When it comes to the mode of giving birth women can decide today whether or not to have anaesthesia during childbirth and if so in what form they should take it. They may often also be given a choice between a natural birth and a Caesarean. In the past infectious illnesses were a threat to our very existence. Today we choose to protect ourselves by inoculations and antibiotics and this means that for the majority of us health has become a norm until the degenerative diseases of the ageing process strike us down. The wisdom of the past, epitomized by one of Jesus' own sayings, took for granted that 'no one by taking thought can add anything to their span of life' (cf. Matt. 6.27). Today we are advised on all sides to take careful thought about 'what we shall eat or what we shall drink' and about the kind of exercise regime we undergo, in order precisely that we may perhaps add to our life span by taking thought about such matters.

Personal autonomy as a challenge to belief in particular providence

It is worth noting that the development of individual autonomy has been controversial for many Christians. It is clear for example from the Prayer Book Catechism that people used to be taught that their position in life was largely determined by their birth situation. Hence they were urged 'To submit myself to all my governors, teachers, spiritual pastors and masters: To order myself lowly and reverently to all my betters: . . . and to do my duty in that state of life, unto which it shall please God to call me.'

The belief that God determined our individual destiny was most marked in the attitude of earlier generations to disease. This comes out most clearly in the form of service recommended for the Visitation of the Sick in the 1662 Prayer Book of the Church of England. In this the priest is required to remind the sick person that 'Almighty God is the Lord of life and death . . . Wherefore, whatsoever your sickness is, know you certainly, that it is God's visitation.' The priest tells the sick person that the illness has either been sent 'to try your patience' or it has been sent to warn the patient to 'correct and amend' whatever it is that the patient has done to 'offend' God. The priest prays either that it will be God's pleasure to restore him or her to the health they formerly enjoyed or that God will take the sick person to dwell with him in life everlasting. The whole service presupposes a picture of God as determining in detail whatever it is that happens to us. It is an understanding of God's relationship with the world which comes to us from a former age and the service in its present format is simply unusable by a priest setting out today to visit a sick person.

The legacy of belief in particular providence

It is true that one legacy of this former belief system can be that when a person is first diagnosed with a terminal illness they may well ask, 'What have I done to deserve this? It's not fair!' Some in such circumstances may seek to 'negotiate' with God for recovery, but almost any contemporary chaplain would seek to reassure the patient that the illness has not been sent by God as any kind of punishment, and that God loves them. It is also the case that the whole ethos of a modern hospital goes flat against any idea that a terminal illness is God-given or that it should be accepted as inevitable. Today there is only one context in which Christian priests and doctors argue that God alone should determine when we die, and that is when they are arguing against the legalization of euthanasia. In every other context it is taken for granted that the doctors should do everything they possibly can do to take charge of the situation. This is shown most vividly when a patient's heart first stops beating. Instantly an alarm will sound and everything possible will be done by the medical staff to resuscitate the patient. Yet logically it could perfectly well be argued that when a person's heart stops beating and their lungs stop breathing this should indicate that that individual had reached the end of their natural God-given life and that God had chosen this moment as the hour of their death. However, a medical team that did take such an approach would rightly be regarded as professionally negligent.

Our society believes, I think correctly, that issues of life and death are a human responsibility. The case for euthanasia or for assisted dying is that we should be consistent in the way we assess the human situation. We should indeed recognize that as long as there remains the possibility for a further extension to a life that the dying person still values, we should do everything in our power to help them fight against their last illness. But equally it seems reasonable to say that when a dying person finds their condition unbearable, and repeatedly asks for assistance to end it all, we should be equally receptive to their wishes. This is why the issue of euthanasia and of assisted dying have come to the fore in our generation.

3

The personal dimension

Why the personal dimension matters

Most people who join voluntary euthanasia societies do so because they were distressed by the way their parents or grandparents suffered during a terminal illness. Having observed this suffering at close hand in a beloved relative they want the law changed so that there can be alternative way of dying. This is certainly true in my own case. I know that anecdotage is not good evidence. I also know that in debates with people who oppose euthanasia it is common to hear accounts of peaceful and pain-free deaths. Nevertheless the fact remains that the fundamental reason why I and others support euthanasia and assisted dying is because of what we have witnessed happening to our nearest and dearest, and it is ultimately because of this that we want the law changed. For us not to mention what are personally the most compelling grounds for our convictions would be a disservice to the debate.

Hans Küng's personal experience

Hans Küng is in a similar situation. He acknowledges that for him personally what was 'decisive' for his attitude to euthanasia was 'the terribly slow process' of his brother's death. Over a process of a year 'one limb after another, one organ after another ceased to function' and eventually 'after days of gasping' his brother finally 'choked on the rising fluid in his lungs'.[1]

The deaths of my grandparents

My own convictions about euthanasia began with the death of my father's elderly parents and have been strengthened by almost every death of which I have had first-hand knowledge. My grandfather died of inoperable stomach cancer. We were warned that there would come a time when he would no longer wish to eat, but that this would probably coincide with a time when the disease had advanced so much that his body would in any case no longer be able to process his food. Gradually he wasted away and slowly died. Because this death took place in the early 1950s his pain was not well controlled and he died a slow and agonizing death. His physical distress was made worse by the fact that during this ordeal he lost his faith in God. This latter circumstance caused my father great concern, because Grandad had always been a most devout and dedicated churchman who had encouraged and supported my father in seeking ordination. My grandfather's death impressed on me at an early stage in life that suffering is not always, or even often, a path to spiritual growth. The Prayer Book service for the Burial of the Dead was much more realistic to pray:

> Suffer us not, at our last hour,
> For any pains of death, to fall from thee.

My paternal grandmother died of senile dementia, which I imagine would have been diagnosed today as Alzheimer's. Towards the end of her life she had no idea who anyone was, including herself. She looked on her husband of over 60 years as a total stranger, and although I saw her every day she always asked, 'Who are you, little boy?' She had no idea that my father was her son, but she noticed his clerical collar, so every time he entered her room Grandma expressed pleasure that the Vicar was kind enough to call to see her. Her faith was the one thing that held her together, or that gave her any happiness. One particular litany of questions impressed itself on me. After a series of questions she would often ask, 'How old am I?' On being told that she was 85 she would always respond, 'Eighty-five! – That means I will be seeing my Saviour soon.' She would appear radiantly happy at this thought. This prompted me to formulate my first childish presentation of a Christian case for euthanasia: 'What Grandma really wants is to die, and go to heaven to be with Jesus. Why don't we let her?'

My mother's mother dropped dead of a heart attack in her sixties and therefore her death did not directly influence my thinking on this issue whereas my mother's father, like my paternal grandfather, died of inoperable stomach cancer. By the time he came to die, however, palliative care had sufficiently advanced that his pain was largely controlled. What he suffered was the gradual diminishment of his life until he was wholly bedridden. The starkest suffering was for his family as we watched him slowly fade away to a living skeleton. As we noted in the previous chapter, in the case of inoperable stomach cancer, all the doctors can do is to ensure that the person is adequately sedated as they gradually starve to death. To provide nourishment artificially until the cancer spread to other organs would simply be to prolong the process of dying in a burdensome way. In such circumstances it would be good if there were the option of a speedier end than that of slow starvation. Given that in the end the only way to avoid the pain is to make the sedation continuous the question does arise, 'In whose interest is life being prolonged under these circumstances?'

My father's death

The worst death was that of my father. He died of prostate cancer over ten years. Despite considerable suffering much of the additional life given to him by a successful operation was beneficial. It was also especially valuable to his family. My father was always grateful that he lived to see his children established in life, and the arrival of his first grandchildren. It was, however, unfortunate that towards the end he was encouraged to undergo a treatment that was both 'burdensome and futile'. These expressions, commonly used in the medical literature, seriously understate the enormity of what can happen. In an American work with the same title as my own book, *Facing Death*, the authors use the word 'torture' to describe the practical impact of 'treatments routinely given to extend the dying process'.[2] That was certainly my father's experience. He even talked of being 'taken to the rack' and said he had 'no idea that there were so many different varieties of pain'. He was not alone, however, in accepting such treatment. According to Sherwin Nuland,

Almost everyone seems to want to take a chance with the slim statistics oncologists give to patients with advanced disease. Usually they
suffer for it, they lay waste their last months for it, and they die
anyway, having magnified the burdens they and those who love them
must carry to the final moments.[3]

My father survived for a couple of years after that treatment. For
most of that time he was either in pain or heavily sedated to avoid
the pain. He suffered more than he needed to suffer because
he wanted to be mentally alert, and found that the painkillers
clouded his mind. He was expected to die in December 1974
and we gathered round to say our final farewells. He gave us
his last advice and blessing and expressed the wish that I and
my mother's sister would stay on in the flat he shared with my
mother until his end, which he felt would be very soon. We could
not do that, and he lived or 'partly lived' till the following July.

Sherwin Nuland notes that:

In ages past, the hour of death was, in so far as circumstances permitted, seen as a time of spiritual sanctity and a last communion
with those left behind. The dying expected this to be so, and it
was not easily denied them. It was their consolation and the consolation of their loved ones for the parting and especially for the
miseries that had very likely preceded it. For many this last communion was the focus not only of the sense that a good death was
being granted them but of the hope they saw in the existence of
God and an afterlife.[4]

I wish that it had been both legally possible and ecclesiastically
encouraged for us to have used modern medicine to restore the
possibility of a Christian deathbed for so faithful a priest. This
was not legally possible nor was it an option my father would
have considered. As his poem that I quote in my dedication of this
book makes clear his theological understanding required that he
accepted his suffering as God's will for him. I shall discuss this
theological understanding of suffering in Chapter 8. But I wish
that an alternative understanding had been available because I
believe it would have been good if my father's wish to say a final
goodbye to us all could have been realized and he had been given

an opportunity to embrace death surrounded by his loved ones and in full assurance of faith. Instead he lingered on and died in his sleep seven months later.

My mother's death

My mother survived my father for 25 years. Despite a major heart attack fairly soon after she was widowed, she made a good recovery and thanks to modern medication was enabled to lead an active life almost into her eighties. She took a degree in history in her late sixties and kept up her historical interests thereafter, with the latest journals and biographies being eagerly read. Living in Highcliffe-on-Sea she swam daily for much of the year as well as enjoying long walks in the New Forest. She loved to welcome her children, grandchildren and great-grandchildren to stay with her as well as enjoying regular foreign holidays. However, in her eighties her health gave way with renewed heart trouble, diabetes, failing sight and hearing, a collapsing spine that caused her intense difficulty in walking, and a wide variety of other ailments. At 86 she asked her doctor and her family to ensure that when she next had a heart attack she should be allowed to die. She was very articulate about this: 'I've had a happy life. It has come to its natural end. It's time for me to go.' Unfortunately, when her heart next failed her, she was brought through its trauma, but only to end up hospitalized in a state of total dependency. At this point she asked for euthanasia. This was because she now found herself in precisely the condition she had sought to avoid by asking not to be given further treatment. Since medical intervention had denied her the natural death that she had asked for she felt that medical intervention should reverse the situation. Since euthanasia is illegal, her request could not be granted, and with 24-hour nursing of the very highest quality her dying was extended for many weeks.

Today, under the Mental Capacity Act, which came into force in 2007, an advance decision not to be treated would have the force of law, and it would be a criminal offence to resuscitate a person who had asked to be allowed to die. So today a person in a comparable position to my mother would not have been resuscitated provided that they had placed their request in writing (which my mother had not done, but would have done if the Act had then existed). This new provision for letting a person die is a significant improvement on the earlier situation. But it will not solve all problems. It remains the case that where a person has not identified the need to make an advance decision an intervention, intended for the best of reasons, might leave a person with an unacceptably low quality of life from which they may wish to be released. It is also the case that allowing a person to die will not prevent the dying process being unacceptably prolonged. I believe that having accepted the right of a person to choose death by declining medical intervention we ought also to accept the right of a person to have their death assisted in its final stages.

The death of my wife's father

The final death to affect me personally was that of my father-in-law who lived next door to me for the last 19 years of his life and was therefore very close. He died of asbestosis contracted through working in the engine-room of a ship during the Second World War. The disease meant a gradual diminishment of his mobility over a period of years. Near the end he could do virtually nothing for himself. As a former naval officer used to being in charge he found total dependency very irksome. His life was a constant struggle for breath, assisted by an oxygen supply that had gradually to be increased as the illness progressed. We all realized that once the maximum level of oxygen delivery had been achieved he would inevitably choke, and die gasping for breath. This meant that we were always cautious about moving up to each new level. My father-in-law was well aware of the fate that awaited him. Repeatedly he would say that his one wish was that he 'would go to sleep one night, and wake up dead the next morning'. This way of putting it may reflect a belief that death would not be his final end, and it might echo a memory of the Prayer Book Psalter that after death I shall 'awake up after thy likeness' and 'shall be satisfied with it' (Psalm 17). Whether or not that is what he meant, his frequently expressed and very rational preference to die in his sleep rather than choke to death is something that an assisted death could have guaranteed for him. In the end, his wish to die in his sleep was granted by a wholly unexpected internal haemorrhage. If death had followed the normal pattern of an asbestosis death it would have been far more dreadful.

A final reflection

Reflecting on these deaths makes me aware that compared to the nightmarish scenarios described in Sherwin Nuland's *How We Die*, and in Guy Brown's *The Living End*, my relatives were relatively fortunate. For most of their terminal illnesses they were nursed at home and in all cases they were surrounded by loving care. Yet even so it is clear to me that if I were to find myself in one of the situations that they faced I would wish an alternative way out. Like almost all who wish for a Death with Dignity Act in Britain I admit that one powerfully motivating factor is the wish that the law be changed before I have to go through what I saw the generation above me face.

4

Euthanasia as discussed from 'absolutist' perspectives on morality

The difference between absolute and relative values

In debates on the morality of euthanasia it is often the case that participants do not really engage with one another's arguments. This is because the participants may well be working within very different ethical systems. If one believes that moral values are absolute and God-given, one will not be impressed by arguments that presuppose a relativistic approach to ethics and that argue from the perspective of a particular case. If one believes that certain kinds of behaviour are intrinsically evil, one will not take kindly to arguments that seek to justify such behaviour under certain conditions. The dominant approach in both Catholic and Evangelical traditions is to champion an absolute morality whereas a very influential tradition in Humanist circles is a utilitarian morality that insists that in any particular case the balance of good and evil must be weighed in the light of that specific situation.

In ethical theory an absolutist approach to ethics is termed 'deontological' while a relativistic approach is 'consequentialist'. From a deontological perspective it is characteristically argued that euthanasia entails killing another person. Killing people is intrinsically evil. Hence arguments about whether or not in any particular case euthanasia would lessen the sum of human misery is irrelevant to the morality of the deed itself. From this perspective one can have a clear position on what is right and on what is wrong.

From a consequentialist perspective nothing is good or bad in itself. Everything depends on what consequences follow. The key to decide whether an action is right or wrong is to look at what happens as a result of behaving in that way. In the case of euthanasia the question to be decided is whether easing the death of a dying person leads to a diminution of human misery or suffering. If it does, then it could be a justifiable action to take. From this perspective one cannot make sweeping judgements on moral questions but must recognize the complexity of human situations.

In this chapter I propose to examine the foundations of deontological arguments against euthanasia to see if they are really as secure as their proponents believe. In the next I shall explore the debate from a consequentialist position.

Ethics as divine commandments

A very influential Christian tradition sees morality as given to us by God through the Bible as interpreted within the Christian tradition. Evangelical Christians sometimes refer to the Bible as providing the 'maker's instructions' as to how we should behave. This does not mean that all commandments in the Bible are regarded as binding because there has been a long tradition in Christian thought of seeing certain Old Testament laws as belonging to an earlier dispensation. However, the Ten Commandments, including the sixth which states 'Thou shalt not kill' (Exod. 20.13) are seen as permanently authoritative. This can rapidly close down any discussion. 'God says killing is wrong, euthanasia involves killing, therefore euthanasia is wrong.'

In addition to the teaching of the Bible the position of the Roman Catholic Church is completely unequivocal. According to the latest Catechism:

> An act or omission which by, of itself or by intention, causes death in order to eliminate suffering constitutes a murder gravely contrary to the dignity of the human person and to the respect due to the living God, his Creator. The error of judgement into which one can fall in good faith does not change the nature of this murderous act, which must always be forbidden and excluded.[1]

Ethics as obedience to the core principles of Western medicine

For a Christian doctor the almost universal teaching of the Church is backed additionally by the oldest and most respected tradition in Western medicine. This is known as the Hippocratic oath and has been venerated within the medical profession since its initial proclamation by Hippocrates in the fourth century before Christ. It includes the sacred promise that:

> I will prescribe regimens for the good of my patients according to my ability and my judgement and never do harm to anyone. To please no one will I prescribe a deadly drug nor give advice which may cause his death.[2]

Euthanasia as contrary to Natural Law and to the 'moral law within'

The Catholic Church does not base its moral teaching solely on the Bible and the Christian tradition. It also studies Natural Law and asks what kind of behaviour is consonant with the order of nature. It is argued that we have very powerful instincts within us to seek the preservation of our lives. Hence it would seem that suicide is an unnatural act and for one person to kill another at that person's request would seem to go against all our instincts. As Aquinas puts it: 'because everything naturally loves itself, everything keeps itself in being, wherefore suicide is contrary . . . to natural law and to charity'.[3] Immanuel Kant develops a similar argument: 'We shrink in horror from suicide because all nature seeks its own preservation; an injured tree, a living body, an animal does so; how then could man make of his freedom . . . a principle for his own destruction?'[4]

Kant's own ethical theory known as the 'Categorical Imperative' provides a further ground for opposing assisted suicide. According to Kant, in considering the morality of any action we should ask ourselves whether we would like everyone to behave in this way. He suggests we should 'Act only on that maxim through which you can at the same time will that it should become a universal

29

law.'[5] If one ignores the context of responding to the pleas for help from a dying person and simply focuses on the act leading to the termination of another human being's life one can simply argue that killing people is not something any one would wish to will as a universal law and hence euthanasia should be forbidden. Today the deontological tradition has been further strengthened by the popularity of 'virtue ethics' expounded by Alasdair MacIntyre. What is crucial is what sort of behaviour we see as virtuous in itself. Once again if one is generalizing about human behaviour then the preservation of life is normally seen as the act of a virtuous person, while to kill another person would not be something one would characteristically see as a virtuous act.

A summary of the deontological case against euthanasia

People who start from the presumption that moral values are given and that they are absolute are normally far more ready to see euthanasia as simply 'wrong' than people who adopt a consequentialist approach. If the Bible condemns the taking of human life, then it is not for us to oppose this command, particularly as it is backed by 2000 years of Christian teaching and by 24 centuries of medical tradition. Euthanasia also seems to be against nature since human beings characteristically cling to life, and to kill a defenceless human being is not a natural way of behaving. It is also a way of behaving one would not wish to see universalized. Indeed, as we shall see, the strongest argument of all against legalizing euthanasia is that allowing it in particular cases might lead to it becoming a general practice in the care of the dying, and that would be something everyone would find abhorrent. Finally, it must seem far more virtuous to care for the dying rather than simply to kill them. For many Christian activists the question of euthanasia is therefore a non-issue. They believe it is something that their tradition has always forbidden and it is also one that their leaders continue to oppose. Evangelical and Catholic wings within the Church are united on this matter. For both traditions, euthanasia is simply wrong.

Is any questioning of a divine commandment the product of our fallen nature?

Many Christians believe that even to ask the question of whether or not one of God's Ten Commandments is absolute is to repeat the sin of Adam and Eve. One influential tradition of exegesis argues that the temptation of the serpent was precisely to ask: 'Did God say, "You shall not eat of any tree of the garden"?' It was only after Eve had opened up herself to the possibility of questioning the divine law that her senses then led her astray. She noted that the tree was 'good for food, and that it was a delight to the eyes and . . . to be desired to make one wise' (Gen. 3.1, 6). Hence she disobeyed God and ate the fruit. The traditional hermeneutic sees her action as exemplifying the New Testament insight that the root of our fallen nature, and that which separates us from God, is 'the lust of the flesh and the lust of the eyes and the pride of life' (1 John 2.16). All these combine to encourage us to set up our own personal and independent judgement over against the direct command of God.

How does the Old Testament interpret the significance of the sixth commandment?

In the past two centuries Christian scholarship has come to believe that a mode of biblical interpretation that closes down any questioning of traditional teaching is not really true to the Bible itself. If we want to explore whether or not the command 'Thou shalt not kill' implies a belief that terminating a human life is intrinsically wrong in all circumstances, we need to examine the context in which that teaching was given and how that teaching was interpreted within the Bible itself.

What we find is that the absolutist interpretation of biblical commands is nothing like as securely rooted in the teaching of the Bible as is generally supposed. It is indeed true that the sixth of the Ten Commandments says, 'Thou shalt not kill', but if we actually look at the Old Testament law code we immediately realize that the command not to kill was never thought of as an *absolute* command. It was subject to numerous exceptions, some of which seem to modern eyes quite appalling. The most startling is the endorsement of wars of extermination against Israel's enemies in which every man, woman and child was to be killed.[6] The other surprise is how often the death penalty is prescribed. It is invoked for consulting a medium,[7] for gathering twigs on the Sabbath day,[8] for reviling one's parents,[9] for homosexuality,[10] adultery[11] or incest,[12] or even for having sex while the woman is menstruating.[13] Parents had the right to complain to the elders of the city that their son had become a disobedient glutton and a drunkard, and they could thereby have him stoned to death.[14] A priest's daughter who had premarital sex was to be burnt alive.[15] In contrast, a man who flogged his slave-girl to death was not to be punished (provided she didn't actually die during the flogging itself) because 'the loss of his property is punishment enough' (Exod. 21.21). Compared with all these exceptions to the law against killing, the justification of euthanasia would seem a very easy task. What is clear from the long list of capital offences is that the Old Testament law does not forbid killing as such, but what it does do is to forbid murder and it is right to do so. The essence of murder is to take away an innocent person's life against their will, and to thereby deprive that person of all the possibilities that this life affords. That is a wholly different thing from responding to the request of a dying person to help them bring their own suffering to an end.

The relevance of the Hippocratic oath

As a statement of principle the Hippocratic oath remains important. The murderous career of Dr Shipman shows that a general injunction against doctors poisoning their patients is as relevant as ever. But as with the biblical commandment, 'Thou shalt not kill', the Hippocratic oath does not cover all the complexities of end-of-life decision-making in the twenty-first century. The key element in the oath is that the doctor must never 'harm' the patient and must always work for his or her 'benefit'. It is clear that a 'futile' and 'burdensome' treatment can do harm to a patient, whereas to ease the death of someone who is suffering unbearably in the final stages of terminal illness does not. If the patients themselves repeatedly ask for assistance to die, it is clear that such patients see assistance to die as a real 'benefit' to them.

Recognition of the growing complexity of medicine has led medical schools to see the Hippocratic oath as no longer representative of their position. A survey of 27 medical schools in Britain in 1994 found that only three still used the Hippocratic oath in their graduation ceremonies, and only one required the newly qualified doctor to swear it.[16] Globally, it is increasingly being replaced by the Geneva Declaration, initially adopted by the World Medical Association in 1948 and revised thereafter. Unlike the Hippocratic oath, the Geneva Declaration does not refer specifically to either abortion or euthanasia. Instead, it says that the physician shall 'respect the local and national codes of ethics . . . bear in mind the obligation to respect human life . . . and always act in the patient's best interest when providing medical care'.[17] It would be entirely compatible with such a declaration, for a doctor to ease the death of a dying person where the laws of a particular country permitted the doctor to do so.

Can a Bible-believing Christian legitimately choose death for him- or herself?

To many this will seem a strange question, because it is widely believed that 'The Everlasting [has] . . . fixed his canon 'gainst self-slaughter!' Hence the 'calamity of so long life' and of 'the thousand natural shocks that flesh is heir to'[18] must be endured. But this is Shakespeare, speaking through Hamlet. It is not the case that the canonical scriptures forbid suicide. They forbid murder, and hence perhaps by implication suicide, but the implication is not spelt out within the Bible. It was later spelt out by St Augustine who added the gloss 'neither thyself nor another'.[19] But there is nothing in the biblical text itself to justify this extension. As St Augustine well knew, there are biblical suicides that are in no way condemned. The best-known of these is that of Samson who is said to have prayed to God to renew his strength to pull the house of Dagon down upon his head so that he would die with his enemies.[20] St Augustine tried to explain away this self-chosen death as an exceptional case justified by God's 'particular command' given through the spirit within Samson. However, there is nothing in the text to justify this notion of an exceptional command, and if appeal is made to the promptings of our inner spirit presumably any person might make a comparable claim. The truth is that the Hebrew Bible (what Christians commonly call the Old Testament) contains six instances of voluntary death and the Apocrypha contains many more. All such suicides are recorded without any condemnation and indeed appear to be seen as wholly appropriate when a person faced an imminent and degrading death, or was willing to give their own life for the sake of destroying the enemies of their country.

Thus the suicides of King Saul and of his armour-bearer in order to escape the humiliation of capture and mockery are reported without negative comment and their deaths were said to be lamented by the whole of Israel.[21] Eleazur Avaran is said to have 'given his life to save his people and to win himself an everlasting name' by stabbing a war elephant from beneath so it fell on him and killed him as well as the enemies whom it carried.[22] Razis 'fell upon his own sword, preferring to die nobly than to fall into the hands of sinners and suffer outrages unworthy of his noble birth' (2 Macc. 14.41–42). Clearly these are not precise parallels with the assisted suicide of a person dying from terminal illness. However, research into the motivation of those who seek for death under the Death with Dignity Act in Oregon shows that what 80 per cent of them found unbearable was the loss of their dignity through the inescapable humiliations of the dying process.[23] Hence their motivation may not be wholly unlike that of Saul or Razis in seeking a more dignified form of dying. In none of these biblical cases is there any hint of disapproval. In the New Testament we are of course told that Judas Iscariot hanged himself, but this is simply reported without comment, and the woe predicted on Judas was prior to the suicide, not consequential to it.[24]

In the intertestamental period voluntary martyrdom came to be seen as a supreme religious value and in certain circumstances suicide could be seen as 'A Noble Death'. The evidence for this is very thoroughly documented by Arthur Droge and James Tabor in their book of that title.[25] I draw the reader's attention to their careful discussion of the instances of willing martyrdom and suicide in the works of Josephus and Philo. The best known of such instances is of course the mass suicide at Masada which ended the Jewish war of 70–3 CE.

The imitation of Christ

For Christians one foundation for ethical behaviour is the imitation of Christ. Historically he died a cruel death at the hands of his enemies. Yet strangely the Fourth Gospel presents it as the product of Jesus' own choice to lay down his life: 'No one takes it from me, but I lay it down of my own accord' (John 10.18). In one of Jesus' best-loved parabolic images he pictures himself as a good shepherd ready to lay down his life for his sheep. What is often overlooked is that the imagery makes no sense except on the supposition that a caring shepherd would indeed be willing to risk his life to save his sheep.[26] Jesus taught that a readiness to die for another is the ultimate test of true friendship, 'Greater love has no man than this, that a man lay down his life for his friends' (John 15.13). Such sayings are not directly relevant to euthanasia, though it is interesting to recall that these verses came into the mind of Scott in the Antarctic when the dying Captain Oates walked out into the snow to perish quickly and thereby enhance the chances of survival for all his colleagues. What such verses legitimately teach is that death is not the ultimate evil to be avoided at all costs. It is something that can be legitimately embraced as a positive good. The sanctity of life is not a biblical absolute. It is a value that has to be balanced against other values.

St Paul's choice of death

St Paul too is clearly presented as choosing death. In his letter to the Philippians he described the dilemma he felt, 'For to me to live is Christ, and to die is gain. . . . *Yet which I shall choose I cannot tell*' (Phil. 1.22, my italics). In the end he chose to 'finish his course with joy' by going to the death that awaited him in Jerusalem.[27] He felt no concern about this prospect: 'I am already on the point of being sacrificed; the time of my departure has come. I have fought the good fight, I have finished the race, I have kept the faith. Henceforth there is laid up for me the crown of righteousness' (2 Tim. 4.6–8).

The voluntary deaths of early Christian martyrs

Arthur Droge and James Tabor show how influential belief in the 'voluntary' deaths of Jesus and St Paul was among Christians of the first three centuries. St Ignatius urged the importance of an *imitatio mortis Christi*,[28] believing with most second- and third-century Christians that to imitate Christ by choosing a voluntary death by martyrdom or suicide could indeed be 'A Noble Death'. Droge and Tabor also argue that prior to what they call 'The Augustinian reversal' many of the early Christians shared the stoic understanding that a self-chosen death could be a rational act when chosen to avoid intolerable pain or incurable disease.[29]

When speaking of the 'voluntary deaths' of the early Christian martyrs we mean precisely that. In general the Roman authorities followed the course recommended by the Emperor Trajan that Christians were 'not to be sought out' and even if accused and convicted of being Christian they were to be pardoned if they repented and worshipped the Roman gods.[30] Droge and Tabor show that if one examines the records of the early Christian martyrs it becomes apparent that 'very few' had been sought out by the Roman authorities.[31] G. E. M. de Ste Croix says 'nearly twice as many, or more were volunteers'.[32] In other words, they voluntarily gave themselves up to the authorities, thus forcing their own trial and subsequent death. This claim has been vindicated by the careful research into 'radical martyrdom' (where the Christian has sought out death) by Paul Middleton. The most extreme example of this was the occasion when all the Christians of a town handed themselves in to be martyred, and after the first few executions the harassed proconsul, Arrius Antonius, cleared the courts, telling them that if they were all so anxious to die they should find cliffs to throw themselves off, or nooses to hang themselves with.[33]

As well as giving full details of those early Christians who achieved their wish of being martyred by the authorities,

'Eusebius and other early Christian writers mention numerous instances of Christians taking their own lives to procure martyrdom, to avoid apostasy, or to preserve the crown of virginity.'[34] The holy women who chose 'death before dishonour' posed a particular problem for St Augustine because they had become venerated within the Church and crowds flocked to their tombs. As in the case of Samson, St Augustine was forced to argue that they must be exceptional as having had an individual command from God to lay down their lives in this way.[35]

The popularity of radical martyrdom in the first three centuries of the Christian era is not a precise parallel to our present concerns about euthanasia in the context of terminal illness. But it does highlight the fact that the earliest Christian tradition certainly did not see death as a fate to be avoided at all costs, but one that might be legitimately accepted or even sought out for some sufficient cause.

Some biblical perspectives on terminal illness

The question that has to be addressed is whether a swift death at one's own choosing can be legitimate for a Christian when the alternative is a prolonged dying process. From a biblical perspective the most relevant texts here would seem to be those that discuss the relative value of life in the context of terminal illness. Clearly there are abundant verses that speak of the value and worthwhileness of life when one is enjoying health and vigour. In such circumstances the thought of death is very bitter.[36] But when death comes at the end of a long life it is seen as natural and even welcome. For Ecclesiastes 'There is a time to be born and a time to die' (Eccles. 3.2). Ecclesiasticus comments, 'O death, how welcome is your sentence to one who is in need and is failing in strength, very old and distracted over everything; to one who is contrary, and has lost his patience!' (Ecclus. 41.2).

It seems to me entirely appropriate for contemporary Christians to suggest that the success of modern medicine in prolonging our lives re-opens the question St Augustine closed down, of whether once again a death of one's own choosing can be legitimate for a Christian when the alternative is an agonizing, long-drawn-out, and ultimately futile battle with a terminal illness. According to Ecclesiasticus one should 'weep less bitterly for the dead' than for a person who has lost his reason for 'the life of the fool is worse than death' (Ecclus. 22.11). Likewise, faced with terminal illness, there is little point in clinging to life for, 'Death is better than a miserable life, and eternal rest than chronic sickness' (Ecclus. 30.17). My argument is that it is precisely this judgement that a modern Christian should be allowed to make and to act upon in the closing stages of life.

The contribution of Jesus to our ethical understanding

The argument of this chapter so far has been to call into question the absolutizing of the sixth commandment in ways that are alien to its context; to note that no Old Testament suicide is condemned; and to highlight the fact that, prior to St Augustine, Christians held voluntary martyrdom in high regard even if this was by one's own hand. We also noted that for the first three centuries the deaths of Jesus and St Paul were held to have been essentially self-chosen. We now take the question as to what it is that the New Testament sees as the basis for our ethical judgement.

Deontological interpretations of Christianity see it as essentially a command ethic. This is not easy to reconcile with the conflicts Jesus had with the religious authorities of his day. It is salutary to go through the Gospels and note that in almost all cases of dispute the issue was Jesus giving priority to human need over and above the letter of the law, insisting for example that the Sabbath was made for man, not man for the Sabbath.[37] It is also interesting that St Paul saw as the decisive difference between the new Christianity and his upbringing in the 'strictest party' of his former religion[38] that Christians were now free from religious law.[39]

This emphatically does not mean that Jesus had no distinctive ethic. He did. It found expression in his own summary of what was the important law of all and in his 'Golden Rule'. Jesus' summary of the law was:

> You shall love the Lord your God with all your heart, and with all your soul, and with all your mind. . . . You shall love your neighbour as yourself. On these two commandments depend all the law and the prophets. (Matt. 22.37–40)

His 'Golden Rule' was:

> Always treat others as you would like them to treat you: that is the Law and the prophets.

If we seek to apply these principles to medicine we become aware that throughout life our hope is that if we fall ill we will be able to obtain medical help to be restored to life and vitality. On this principle we should seek to ensure that medical treatment is as widely available as possible to all persons suffering any kind of disease or infirmity whether of mind or body. Doctors and nurses who minister to the sick in this way are widely recognized by Christians as genuine agents and embodiments of God's providential love. Christians often describe the professions of medicine and nursing as 'vocations', that is, jobs to which people may feel called by God to undertake for the good of humanity. When we fall terminally ill our wishes usually change. Six recent opinion polls show that between 81 per cent and 87 per cent of the population would like to have medically assisted suicide legalized so that if they find themselves suffering unbearably in the final stages of terminal illness they can be helped.[40] If we believe that people should be treated as they themselves wish to be treated, then this is what we as Christians ought to support. This is even more true for members of the medical profession.

Assisted suicide and the medical profession

The suicide rate is far higher among doctors than among the general public. No doubt many factors contribute to this, but at least one is the fact that they know the implications of terminal illness, and have the knowledge and means to release themselves from it. Dr Michael Irwin, a former Medical Director of the United Nations, claims that 'many physicians and nurses have private arrangements that they will hasten each others' deaths should they ever be unfortunate enough to resemble the condition of some of their patients'.[41] For doctors who have made such 'arrangements', the legalizing of assisted suicide would not only protect their colleagues from possible serious repercussions, it would also enable such doctors to give to their patients the treatment they wish for themselves.

Since I first quoted Dr Irwin's comment in print I have been interested to note that several doctors have confided in me that they have indeed made such arrangements. Baroness Warnock and Dr Elisabeth Macdonald have discovered the same phenomenon. They think it is of moral interest, 'that highly ethical and humane physicians have been known to assist their colleagues and their loved ones to have a more merciful death in contrast to their normal practice with the majority of their patients'.[42] They note that, writing in the *Journal of the American Medical Association*, Dr K. L. Vaux makes a comparable point, 'That physicians and nurses would request euthanasia for their colleagues or would assist their loved one to have a more merciful death . . . says something about the moral nature of the act.'[43] What it says to me is that if doctors would extend to their patients the treatment they wish for themselves and their families, they would literally be following Jesus' Golden Rule.

There is little that is 'natural' about a modern death

I noted earlier the argument against euthanasia based on Natural Law and also the argument against it on the basis of Kant's 'Categorical Imperative'. However, neither is as secure as might first appear. For there is nothing 'natural' about most modern deaths. Guy Brown points out that 'We may think that chronic death from old age is "natural" while acute death of the young is somehow unnatural. Of course the exact opposite is the case. Death from old age is extremely rare in wild animals and was rare in humans until one hundred years ago.'[44] Today two of the most likely venues for our death will be either an intensive care unit, or in a hospice or palliative care ward. Neither offers much hope of a 'natural' end. According to Sherwin Nuland,

> treatment decisions are sometimes made at the end of life that propel a person willy nilly into a series of worsening miseries from which there is no extrication – surgery of questionable benefit and high complication rate, chemotherapy with severe side effects and uncertain response and prolonged periods of intensive care beyond the point of futility.[45]

Guy Brown paints an equally gloomy picture:

> Frail withered bodies are plugged into virile machines via a forest of tubes and wires. As the body starts to pack in individual organs or body functions fail. Outside the hospital this would lead to death but in the ICU the organ's function may be replaced by a machine . . . there then comes a stage . . . when respiration and circulation fail . . . nowadays this is the cue for the specialist resuscitation teams to attempt resuscitation, via heart massage, defibrillators and insulin therapy . . . Keeping people alive in intensive care is massively expensive in terms of money, machinery, time and effort, so ultimately the machine will be turned off and the patient will die.

Brown notes that Mervyn Singer, Professor of Intensive Care Medicine at University College London, caused embarrassment to his colleagues by acknowledging that the reason 'most people finally die in intensive care units is not because the body gives up, but because the medics get bored . . . and/or decide to conserve resources'.[46] I noted earlier that the case against euthanasia from the perspective of Natural Law was that euthanasia was 'an unnatural act' and one that 'would seem to go against all our instincts'. I suggest that the intensive care scenario described by Drs Nuland and Brown is even more 'unnatural' and even more 'against our instincts'.

Death in palliative care is very different and far more humane than this. In Chapter 8 I shall discuss how much the best palliative care can do to ease our passing. For our present purposes, however, I simply note that it by no means offers what would traditionally be thought of as a 'natural death' or the kind of death which used to be discussed in classic works like Jeremy Taylor's *Holy Dying*.[47] For many of us death in a hospice will have been preceded by a long period of continuous sedation. According to Dr Julia Lawton's account in *The Dying Process*, 'few who die in a hospice today have the capacity to prepare psychologically or spiritually for death. Many patients died either in extended sleep, in a coma, heavily sedated, or in extreme confusion or pain.'[48]

Could euthanasia offer a more natural end?

If these are the alternatives that many of us will have to face, would it really be less 'natural' to prefer the hemlock supplied by non-Hippocratic physicians in Ancient Greece,[49] or its equivalent in modern barbiturates? These could readily be made available if physicians were allowed to help us in this way when pain or suffering becomes unbearable. And, taking up the challenge of the Categorical Imperative, could we not affirm that, 'yes', it would be desirable if such an end were universally available to any human being who was facing unbearable suffering in the final stages of a terminal illness.

5

Euthanasia from a consequentialist perspective

Bishop Butler's 'Christian empiricism'

While the majority of those who hold to a deontological understanding of ethics (those who see moral commands as given) are opposed to euthanasia, most people who adopt a consequentialist theory of ethics are far more open to the possibility that euthanasia could sometimes be justifiable. Within the Anglican tradition the most influential form of consequentialism has been the Christian empiricism classically formulated by Bishop Joseph Butler in 1726 when he preached *Fifteen Sermons* in the Rolls Chapel in London to a congregation of eminent judges and lawyers. Butler argued that there are essentially two ways of doing ethics. One way starts from a theoretical evaluation based on abstract principles that assumes we know in advance of any real investigation that 'vice is contrary to the nature and reason of things'. The alternative way that Butler embraced was to root morality in an investigation of 'what the particular nature of man is' and 'what course of life corresponds best to this nature'.[1] In such an investigation we will not be committed to any particular theory about human nature but will seek to discover what patterns of behaviour actually lead to human fulfilment and satisfaction, both as individuals and as members of society. This empirical approach Butler believes is best 'adapted to a fair mind; and is more easily applicable to the several particular relations and circumstances of life'.[2]

Butler was conscious that one of the enormous difficulties of trying to base morality on a sacred text was the extent to which conditions of life had changed since biblical times. He was persuaded that not only could one not simply read off ethical

43

commands from the Old Testament law codes but that this principle could also be applied to the New Testament. As he wrote:

> The Letters in the New Testament have all of them a particular
> reference to the condition and usages of the Christian world at the
> time they were written. Therefore as they cannot be thoroughly
> understood, unless that condition and those usages are known and
> attended to so further though they be known, yet if they be dis-
> continued or changed exhortations, precepts and illustrations of
> things, which refer to such circumstances now ceased or altered,
> cannot at this time be urged in that manner, and with that force
> which they were to the primitive Christians.[3]

In many ways this was a remarkable comment to have made in
1726. Since then conditions of life have changed vastly more and
it does indicate that to address the new problems that have arisen
from modern medicine's ability to prolong the dying process
requires new approaches to how we handle scriptural teaching. As
we shall see Butler believed that the principles underlying Jesus'
teaching were of permanent importance, though the way those may
be applied will differ from age to age.

As a bishop of the Anglican Church Butler did of course
believe that he could learn from the Bible and the tradition of the
Church as well as conscience and reason, but all these must be related to the knowledge that can come from detached and informed
investigation into all the facts available to us about the human
condition. 'Nothing can be more useful than to see things as they
really are.'[4] According to Professor D. M. MacKinnon, Butler's
empiricism is 'the appeal to fact, to what we know of ourselves
and . . . a readiness always to sacrifice the nicety of theoretical
construction to the actuality of human behaviour'.[5]

Butler believed that on the basis of appeal to facts one could
justify what lies at the heart of Christian ethics. Happiness is the
goal that almost all humans seek yet it is an observable fact of
life that if one really wants to be happy it is fatal to have that end
constantly in view. The happiest people are actually those who
are occupied with activities that they feel to be honourable and
useful while those who have nothing but their own pleasure to

consider are often among the most wretched. 'That character we call selfish is not the most promising for happiness.' Consequently, 'immoderate self-love does very ill consult its own interests'.[6] It is as clear 'that we were made for society and to promote the happiness of society; as that we were intended to take care of our own life and health and private good'.[7] Butler believed that the heart of Christian ethics is to take seriously Jesus Christ's own summary of the commandments, namely, 'you shall love your neighbour as yourself' (Matt. 22.39). He believed that this principle of the love of the neighbour can be the guide to all ethical judgement and he proposed that if one follows Jesus Christ's Golden Rule (also taught by Confucius), 'Always treat others as you would like them to treat you',[8] then you have a realistic and workable foundation for ethics.

The influence of Butler's empiricism

Butler's empirical approach to ethics has been a dominant influence in Anglican thought ever since he wrote. In particular it used to be characteristic of the approach of the Church of England Council for Moral Welfare and its successor the Board of Social Responsibility of the Church of England. During the 1950s and 60s these bodies wrote reports on homosexuality, abortion and divorce which in each case foreshadowed subsequent legislation by the British Government.[9] During the 1960s homosexual behaviour between consenting adults in private was legalized, the prohibition of abortion was removed and the divorce laws were greatly liberalized. Church leaders were also heavily involved in other 'permissive legislation' under which attempting to commit suicide ceased to be a criminal offence, censorship of literature and theatre was abolished and capital punishment done away with. In all these cases the Anglican Church leadership sought to change the discussion away from theoretical analysis of whether or not the former position was intrinsically right or wrong. Instead they shifted the debate entirely on to consideration of the harmful consequences of the earlier legal position.

In the discussion on homosexuality the discussion focused on the evil of people being exposed to blackmail; the debate on abortion focused on the plight of women suffering from botched abortions performed by unqualified amateurs; and the debate on suicide pointed out that people who attempted to commit suicide needed help not punishment. In all cases a mass of empirical data was collected to give clear evidence of the consequences of existing legislation as compared with the likely consequences of change.

This whole approach to ethical questions does not mean that moral judgements cannot be made. The Board of Social Responsibility in the Church of England was always clear that the ideal of a life-long marriage remains the Christian goal. Likewise it believed that abortion was a tragedy that needed serious justification. But what the Board was also clear about was that the reality of individual situations also requires recognition. Marriages do irretrievably break down and, in a variety of circumstances, such as when the mother's life is at risk, abortion would be the right choice in a particular situation. What matters is to acknowledge the reality of the human situation and to seek what is the most loving thing to do in the circumstance in which the individual finds him- or herself.

Situation ethics

Mentioning the importance of always looking at the realities of the human situation leads immediately into the second kind of consequentialist ethic: the situation ethics of Joseph Fletcher. Fletcher argued that throughout the Gospels we see Jesus always putting the command of love over all other laws. Almost all the conflicts described in the New Testament between Jesus and the Scribes and Pharisees centred on Jesus' claim that sins could always be forgiven and a fresh start made and that in all cases religious laws existed for the benefit of human beings, not the other way round. What is distinctive about Jesus' own teaching was the way he related everything to the situation of the individual. Hence the one question to be asked in all contexts is simply 'what is the most loving thing to do in this situation?' If one truly loves one's fellow human being as oneself then, as Jesus said, this is to fulfil the law.[10] Applying the law of love to a person suffering unbearably in the final stages of a terminal illness and asking for assistance to die it would seem apparent that in that situation the most loving thing to do is to accede to that request.

Utilitarianism

The final consequentialist ethic is the best known and that is the utilitarian one. From a utilitarian perspective the question to be asked is always what course of action will maximize human happiness. Because it was initially put forward by Jeremy Bentham and James Mill (John Stuart Mill's father) as an alternative to a deontological understanding of Christian ethics, utilitarianism is often seen as an alternative to Christian morality.[11] But as John Stuart Mill pointed out, if one takes Jesus' teaching 'by their fruits you shall know them' (Matt. 7.17–20), it can be argued that he himself valued a consequentialist ethic and was adopting the essence of a utilitarian position.[12] If we apply the test of the 'greatest happiness of the greatest number' it would seem that since over 80 per cent of people believe that their happiness would be enhanced if euthanasia were legalized, the law should be changed to reflect their wishes.

Thinking through the implications of a consequentialist approach to the question of euthanasia or assisted dying, it becomes apparent that at least on the basis of the situation of the dying individual a strong case can be made for helping that individual out. The context within which assisted dying is being discussed is the context of a terminally ill person enduring unbearable suffering and repeatedly asking for assistance to die. If you apply the principle of loving your neighbour as yourself and treating people as you would wish to be treated yourself a strong case can be established on an individualistic basis for helping that individual out. From the point of view of situation ethics the issue is even clearer. Anyone in that situation should be helped. Likewise from a utilitarian perspective there is clearly a prima facie case for assisting the patient to die.

The application of consequentialism to individual 'hard cases'

Almost all ethicists who apply consequentialist modes of thinking to their moral judgements accept that there are cases where euthanasia or assisted dying would be an appropriate response to the needs of a particular individual. Thus the Church of England Board for Social Responsibility in their 1975 report *On Dying Well* recognized that:

> There are bound to be cases in which any of us who is honest with himself and asks 'What do I wish that men should do to me in this particular situation?' would answer 'Kill me'. We have already mentioned such unusual cases [men trapped in blazing gun turrets . . . wounded who face death by torture if left on the battlefield] in which many of us would wish to have our deaths hastened so that the manner of them might be less unbearable. Thus a direct application of the teaching of Jesus (about loving our neighbour as ourselves) to these cases would legitimize at least some instances of euthanasia.[13]

A similar initial perspective was taken by the House of Lords Committee on Medical Ethics that was chaired by Lord Walton in 1994. Many members of that committee were deeply impressed by the arguments for legalizing euthanasia. They recognized that many people suffer 'intolerable pain or indignity' in their terminal illness and they acknowledged 'that there are individual cases in which euthanasia may be seen by some to be appropriate'. Consequently, 'they gave much thought' to the consideration that 'the individual is best able to decide what manner of death is fitting to the life which has been lived'.[14]

Why both the Church of England and the House of Lords rejected euthanasia

Despite these considerations both the Church of England Board for Social Responsibility in 1975 and the House of Lords Committee on Medical Ethics in 1994 ultimately came down against changing the law. In the case of the Board for Social Responsibility the principal worry was the impact that changing the law on euthanasia might have on public attitudes towards vulnerable people. In the case of Lord Walton's committee the worry was to devise a watertight law that could only be applied in what were clearly 'hard cases' and that would avoid 'serious and widespread repercussions' that they felt would inevitably follow from an Act which would 'weaken society's prohibition of intentional killing.[15]

The way 'permissive legislation' in the sixties had unforeseen impacts

One central concern is that permissive legislation tends to change the climate of thought and behaviour in such a way as to lead to consequences very different from those originally intended. Christians opposed to legislation permitting euthanasia are particularly sensitive in this regard. They are well aware that, as already noted, the Church of England Board for Social Responsibility and comparable Nonconformist groups had issued a succession of reports 'arguing for changes in the *laws* relating to homosexual practice, abortion and divorce which closely foreshadowed the legislation subsequently passed'.[16] But they also know that the impact of these laws was very different from what had been foreshadowed when the changes were urged.

The impact of de-criminalizing homosexuality

Those Church bodies who gave testimony to the Wolfenden Committee on homosexuality thought solely in terms of behaviour between 'consenting adults in private'. Their motivation was to stamp out the incidences of people being privately blackmailed. They never envisaged the possibility of the public 'outing' of homosexuality, or of television drama in which it might be presented as commonplace. It did not occur to them that within a generation homosexuals might be candidates for appointment as bishops.

Liberalizing divorce law

The authors of the Anglican Report *Putting Asunder* of 1966[17] did not foresee the explosion in divorce that subsequently followed the Divorce Reform Act of 1969. They were concerned that sometimes, without necessarily there being any 'fault' on either side, some marriages did 'irretrievably break down'. It did not occur to them that within a generation 40 per cent of marriages might do so.

The unforeseen expansion of abortion

Most significantly of all, Christian support for abortion law reform, typified by the Board for Social Responsibility's report *Abortion: An Ethical Discussion*,[18] thought solely in terms of 'hard cases'. This was also true of David Steel whose decision to introduce a bill allowing abortion stemmed from his reading of that report.[19] Christians could see a justification for abortion when the mother's life was in serious peril, or when there was a real risk of gross abnormality in the foetus, and they were happy to support the legislation. Supporters of the bill in 1967 did not imagine that 30 years later a briefing paper, *Abortion and the Church of England*, sent to the diocesan bishops on 14 April 1997 would show that since the 1967 Abortion Act only 0.004 per cent of abortions have actually been carried out to save the life of the mother, and only 1.5 per cent have been performed to prevent 'serious foetal handicap'.[20]

Likewise what was never foreseen was that legislation to allow abortion in 'hard cases' would lead to 200,000 legal abortions a year. No one in 1967 would have believed that within 40 years we would reach a situation where, according to a report in the *Journal of the Royal Society of Medicine*, '22% of conceptions end in abortion . . . induced abortion is now experienced by 35–40% of women by the time they reach 45, and is the most common gynaecological procedure carried out on fit young women . . . Currently 32% of women having abortions have had an abortion in the past.'[21]

The fear that a similar kind of procedural deterioration might apply in the case of euthanasia is undoubtedly the strongest argument against legislating for it. But is this fear justified? Margaret Otlowski believes that the free availability of abortion

> most certainly cannot be taken as evidence of a likely slide from
> voluntary to non-voluntary or involuntary euthanasia if the practice

were to be legalized. Such a claim could only be made if there were evidence that the liberalization of abortion law so as to allow the practice in certain circumstances at a woman's request had led to abortions being performed on women without their consent. This is simply not the case, so the 'abortion analogy' does not hold up to scrutiny as a serious objection to the legalisation of active voluntary euthanasia.[22]

Against Otlowski, however, we must urge that the real parallel came at the earlier stage; the legislation permitting abortion in a number of carefully defined 'hard cases' had led to abortion 'at a woman's request' and this had *not* been intended by the legislators. In the analogy with euthanasia the fear is that legislation intended to relate to cases of unbearable suffering in terminal illness might lead to 'euthanasia on demand' and here the parallel does exist.

The seriousness of 'procedural deterioration'

By far the strongest argument against legalising euthanasia is the concern about how a change in the law might bring about a change in public attitudes to the sick and the dying. This is technically known as the problem of 'procedural deterioration' and more colloquially as 'sliding down a slippery slope'. Robin Gill prefers to talk of not 'crossing a line'.[23] He believes it is of the utmost importance that we keep a clearly drawn line between euthanasia and assisted dying on the one hand and allowing people to die and providing pain relief that may have the side effect of shortening life on the other. It is evident that doctors attach great significance to these distinctions and that many share Gill's concern that this is a line that should not be crossed.

The really deep fear about allowing euthanasia in any circumstances is that we simply do not know the impact such a change might have. This fear is clearly expressed in a joint submission from the Church of England House of Bishops and the Catholic Bishops' Conference to the Select Committee on the Assisted Dying Bill. In this submission the bishops said of the Joffe Bill to allow assisted dying:

To take this step would fundamentally undermine the basis of law and medicine and undermine the duty of the state to care for vulnerable people. It would risk a gradual erosion of values in which over time the cold calculation of the costs of caring properly for the ill and the old would loom large. As a result many who are ill or dying would feel a burden to others. The right to die would become a duty to die.[24]

At a more popular level Tom Wright, the Bishop of Durham, has claimed that the lobby behind the Bill believed that 'we have a right to kill surplus old people'.[25] The Conservative MP Ann Widdecombe claims that 'Reports from the Disability Rights Commission, Disability Awareness in Action, and other bodies show that increasing numbers of disabled and sick people are frightened to be admitted to hospital because of the euthanasia campaign'.[26]

The worries of medical bodies

Concern about the impact of allowing euthanasia is felt by many organizations. The American College of Physicians is worried that if euthanasia were permitted 'the sick, the elderly, the poor, ethnic minorities and other vulnerable groups . . . might come to be further discounted by society, or even to view themselves as unproductive and burdensome and on that basis "appropriate" candidates for assistance with suicide'. The College also believed that 'patients with dementia, disabled persons . . . and those confronting costly chronic illness' would be placed at risk. This concern was shared by the British Medical Association, which likewise believed that legalizing euthanasia would 'put vulnerable people in the position of feeling they had to consider precipitating the end of their lives'.[27]

What happened in Nazi Germany

For many people the fear of enforced euthanasia is not a theoretical one. They believe we should learn from what happened in Germany during the 1940s. Hans Küng acknowledges that 'it is estimated that on the basis of a secret decree of Adolf Hitler, from 1 September 1939 to August 1941 between 60,000 and 80,000 physically or mentally ill people were killed in special killing institutions'.[28] Nigel Biggar believes that this still carries warnings for us today. He cites the argument used by Leo Alexander during the Nuremberg doctors' trial:

> Whatever proportion these [Nazi] crimes finally assumed, it became evident to all who investigated them that they had started from small beginnings. The beginnings at first were a subtle shift in emphasis in the basic attitude of physicians. It started with the acceptance of the attitude, basic in the euthanasia movement, that there is such a thing as a life not worthy to be lived. This attitude in its early stages concerned itself merely with the severely and chronically sick. Gradually the sphere of those included in his category was enlarged to encompass the socially unproductive, the ideologically unwanted, the racially unwanted and finally all non-Germans. But it is important to realize that the infinitely small wedged-in lever from which this entire trend of mind received its impetus was the attitude towards the non-rehabilitable sick.[29]

The significance of the Nazi experience

Nigel Biggar acknowledges that this quotation from the Nuremberg doctors' trial is somewhat tendentious, and that one might want to quarrel with the final sentence. It is also, I suggest, historically inaccurate to suggest that the Holocaust began with a negative attitude towards the non-rehabilitable sick. Hitler's anti-Semitism and his low estimation of non-Aryan races goes back at least as far as *Mein Kampf* in 1925. The roots of Nazism lie in the belief that you can regard some human beings as 'subhuman', and the primary targets of that belief were the Jews. What mattered to Hitler was the extermination of Jews, and incidentally the extermination of other groups such as Gypsies and homosexuals. The so-called 'euthanasia' campaign towards the chronically sick and disabled was a sideshow for Hitler, and one which he abandoned when concern inside Germany became vocal. By contrast, the extermination of the Jews remained a priority right up to the final collapse of the Nazi state.

Biggar is right to argue that elements in Nazi thinking on many matters had antecedents in the Weimar Republic (and I suggest in much earlier German thought).[30] For example, Biggar notes that a 1925 survey inside Germany showed that 73 per cent of parents would approve of the 'painless curtailment of the life of their child if experts showed it was suffering from incurable idiocy'.[31] In terms of German legislation, however, there was no 'slippery slope'. Hitler simply issued a murderous decree. It is therefore wrong to suggest that the German experience under the Nazis is relevant to the contemporary debate. Perhaps the most resolutely hostile person to the concept of assisted dying, Baroness Finlay is adamant that what happened under the Nazis has nothing whatever to do with euthanasia. She states that talk of 'involuntary euthanasia' in the Nazi camps is 'a travesty of the truth . . . That was not euthanasia, that was mass murder'.[32] From a totally different perspective, Lord Joffe protests that for the *Catholic Times* to use a photograph of children murdered by the Nazis as part of their propaganda against his Bill was 'a disgrace'. Mary Warnock is in full agreement with Joffe on this point.[33] The only relevance of the Third Reich to our discussions is that it reminds us of the fragility of our veneer of civilization, and to that extent strengthens the worries of those who believe that any alteration of the law against euthanasia may have unforeseen effects.

The difficulty of foreseeing all consequences

Starting from consideration of what is best for each individual, working on the principle of loving one's neighbour as oneself, and considering the life situation of the dying person, then, a consequentialist ethic would appear to be wholly supportive of voluntary euthanasia. Remember that in this book we are only considering the situation of an individual who is suffering unbearably in the final stages of a terminal illness and who wants assistance to die in order to bring that suffering to an end.

If we explore consequences from the perspective of society, however, the situation is less clear cut. Individuals are not isolated from society and it is apparent that making changes to the ethical framework within which people make decisions can have unpredictable consequences. We saw that vividly in the case of homosexual and divorce law reform and even more so in the case of abortion. It is also true of many other moral issues. When the jury decided that *Lady Chatterley's Lover* as a work of literature written by one of the early twentieth century's most distinguished novelists ought to be published, they did not intend to permit virtually any pornography to be published. Yet that consequence did in fact flow from their decision. Similarly, when Marie Stopes wrote *Married Love* or when people campaigned for family planning, they did not foresee that many highly educated women would plan for a family of one or none, or that pre-marital sex would become almost universal in modern society. It is therefore legitimate for opponents of euthanasia to seek assurance that permitting euthanasia in 'hard cases' does not undermine the sanctity of life in other contexts.

The difficulty of restricting euthanasia to one group only

An awareness of the legitimacy of the concerns about 'sliding down a slippery slope', 'crossing a line' or suffering 'procedural deterioration' has prompted Dignity in Dying to insist on the need for careful safeguards in any proposal for legalizing euthanasia. According to Carmen Dupont, its Policy and Information Officer,[34] Dignity in Dying 'is campaigning for a change in the law to allow terminally ill, mentally competent adults the right to have an assisted death, subject to a range of safeguards'. I acknowledge that it might reasonably be argued that this is too restrictive. After all people who lack 'competence' might equally suffer unbearably in the final stages of their terminal illness. Why should they be denied assistance to die when they have the added hardship of suffering from mental confusion on top of all their other ills? Equally, people can suffer unbearably and may long for assistance to die even though they are not terminally ill. There is also the predicament of the person who has recently been diagnosed with a terminal illness that is likely to develop over many years, and what the patient finds most 'unbearable' is the thought of a decade of gradual disintegration. Consider the position of the newly diagnosed Alzheimer's patient. For such persons it is the early days of the illness that can be the hardest to bear, for at that point they are still aware of their increasing diminishment and the impact this is beginning to have on their loved ones; whereas in the latter stages they may have no consciousness of what their situation really is.

Opponents of euthanasia argue that these factors are precisely why euthanasia should not be allowed at all, because once it is allowed for the competent ill person in the final stages of terminal illness, pressure for extending it to these other categories will inevitably follow. But it is wrong to oppose something for fear of something else if in fact it is possible to exclude the other by careful drafting. There is a case for saying that competent, suffering people, near death, are a distinct category. This is because 'respect for personal autonomy' is one strong argument for allowing euthanasia and sadly people who lack 'competence' lack that essential autonomy and would have to have a decision made on their behalf. That changes the situation radically. Likewise, people who are suffering unbearably, but who are not terminally ill, can reasonably be denied assistance to die because of the real possibility that they will come through their distress and find again the possibility of worthwhile life. In the case of the newly diagnosed Alzheimer's sufferer it is always possible that in the course of the ten years or more that the disease will take to kill them some new treatment might be found that would alleviate their situation. Stem cell research offers at least some possibilities in this direction. In the meantime, since the passing of the Mental Capacity Act in 2007, newly diagnosed Alzheimer's sufferers can give a legally binding Advance Directive that they are not to be given antibiotics in the event that they contract a lesser illness such as pneumonia.

The case for focusing exclusively on the suffering and competent terminally ill

In the debates in the House of Lords on the Assisted Dying for the Terminally Ill Bill virtually no one opposed what Lord Joffe was actually proposing. All the opposition was focused on fears of what might happen later. That was very sad. Given that there could have been a consensus that in the case of the competent, suffering, dying person euthanasia could be justified then it should have been allowed. The Bill was so hedged around with safeguards that no 'sliding' was possible. If, following years of experience of the workings of such a bill, people in the future wanted euthanasia extended to some other category, that would have to be a wholly new decision to be addressed by a quite new bill.

The safeguards in Lord Joffe's Bill

The first thing to note is that the title of the Bill was The Assisted Dying for the Terminally Ill Bill. Terminal illness was defined as an illness in which the patient has six months or less to live. This means that people with a non-terminal illness, elderly people who were not terminal, and people with disabilities who were not terminal were excluded from the Bill's provisions. 'Assisted dying' was the subject of the Bill rather than euthanasia. This means that doctors could prescribe life-ending medication to their patients but they would not themselves be able to administer it. Patients would have to take the medication themselves. This means that right up to the last moment the decision to die would have to be the personally chosen decision of the patient.

Because respect for individual autonomy was an important foundation of the Bill it excluded all people who lacked mental competency to decide for themselves. Hence, no one under 18 could possibly have applied no matter how ill they might have been. This also means that there would no question of sufferers from dementia or Alzheimer's being subject to the Bill. The Bill provided that in any case of doubt about the patient's mental competency there would have to be a referral to a consultant psychiatrist or a clinical psychologist.

The patient must be suffering unbearably and there must be no doubt that they were in the final stages of a terminal illness and that there were no realistic possibilities of recovery. The patient must make persistent, well-informed and voluntary requests for assistance to die. Two independent doctors must assess the patient's condition and satisfy themselves that the request is well-informed, persistent and voluntary and that the patient does indeed meet all the Bill's criteria.

Because 'unbearable suffering' was an important ground of the patient's application the Bill insisted that the patient must have a consultation with a palliative care expert who could explain how appropriate palliative care might alleviate the suffering and how the patient could best obtain such care.

The patient would need to have made at least two oral and one written request for assistance to die. To ensure that this really was the patient's own decision, two independent witnesses who were connected neither with the patient's family nor the hospital must witness the written request and one of these independent witnesses must be a solicitor. This latter provision was to ensure that this was the patient's own settled and firm choice.

The Bill provided a waiting period of at least 14 days for the patient to reflect and possibly reconsider the application and the patient could orally revoke the request at any time. Since in the end the patient must take the medication for themselves there would be the possibility right up to the last moment for a change of heart.

The Bill also carried safeguards for doctors and hospices. No doctor who had conscientious objections to these procedures would be required to participate in any way and indeed would be under no obligation to refer the patient on to another doctor. Any hospice could decide to forbid assisted dying for patients in its care. Throughout the whole operation the autonomy of both doctors and patient must be respected. The precise wording of the conscientious objection clause states:

> No person is under any duty to participate in any diagnosis, treatment or other action to which they have a conscientious objection. Furthermore, no hospice, hospital, nursing home, clinic or other health care establishment is under any obligation to permit an assisted death on their premises.

All the provisions of the Bill can be consulted on the internet.[35] It is believed by Lord Joffe and by supporters of Dignity in Dying that the provisions of the Bill were sufficient enough to have prevented any 'sliding' away from an assisted death restricted absolutely to competent people who were suffering unbearably in the final stages of a terminal illness and who were repeatedly asking for assistance to die. It seems to me that in these strictly limited circumstances it would be entirely appropriate for followers of Jesus Christ to share his concern for individual suffering, and to treat these dying people in the way in which they begged to be treated.

6

Does assisted suicide imply presumption, ingratitude or despair towards God?

Suicide as deserting one's post and rushing unbidden into God's presence

Historically suicide was seen as a sin reflecting either presumption or despair in relation to God. Because Christians used to believe quite literally that, as Aquinas put it, 'God alone has authority to decide about life and death',[1] it was believed that any suicide was an act of presumption in which a person made for him- or herself a decision that rightly should only be made by God. According to William Blackstone's *Commentaries on the Laws of England*, the spiritual offence of which a suicide is guilty consists of: 'invading the prerogative of the Almighty, and rushing into his immediate presence uncalled for'.[2] Immanuel Kant wrote:

> A suicide opposes the purposes of his Creator; he arrives in the other world as one who has deserted his post; he must be looked on as a rebel against God . . . Human beings are sentinels on earth and may not leave their posts until relieved.[3]

In commenting on such texts it is crucial that we are doing so only in the specific context of considering the validity of assisting suicide in the final stages of terminal illness. In other contexts one can see the validity of such objections to suicide. For a person prematurely to kill themselves at a time of temporary depression is a great tragedy. It is entirely right that any society should seek to discourage and counsel against the practice of suicide in such situations. It is also entirely appropriate for a religious believer to hold that a person who commits suicide outside the context of terminal illness has failed to live out on earth the purposes for which God created that person. But these are not the kind of suicides we are currently discussing. We are talking only about people who have come to a terminal condition. They are already dying and they ask for help to make their dying more bearable to them.

Terminal illness could well be understood as a divine summons

To liken the assisted suicide of a dying person to that of a deserter abandoning his or her post while under attack seems most inept. Given belief in any kind of providential order one might conclude that the onslaught of terminal illness was itself the clearest indication that could be given of a divine intention to recall one to another station. As David Hume put it in his classic essay 'On Suicide', 'whenever pain and sorrow so far overcome my patience, as to make me tired of life, I may conclude that I am recalled from my station in the clearest and most express terms'.[4] In the Bible, Job reached the same conclusion and in speech after speech describes the symptoms of his various illnesses as the harbingers of the death he longs for. 'Death would be better than these sufferings of mine . . . I have no desire to live.'[5] The testimony of Job is an important biblical witness to an accepting attitude towards death and should not be discounted because of the Epilogue providing a 'happy ending' to all Job's misfortunes and giving him a wholly fanciful additional lease of life.[6] W. A. Irwin shows in his commentary on Job that there is a very high level of agreement among biblical scholars that the Epilogue was not the work of the original author and was only added subsequently.[7] That ending makes a nonsense both of the seriousness of the discussion of suffering throughout the book and of the religious importance of Job's final acceptance of his position and of his submission to God's will.

Plato, who in general believed suicide to be wrong, recognized an important exception: 'it is not unreasonable to say that we must not put an end to ourselves until God sends some compulsion'.[8] It would seem entirely reasonable to see terminal illness as providing precisely that 'compulsion' that could prompt a life-ending decision. Indeed one could reasonably argue that a person opting for euthanasia in the context of terminal illness was deciding at long last to respond to the divine summons. Almost all who seek for assistance in ending their lives have previously spent many years doing everything possible to delay death. Rather than the scene imagined by Blackstone of a person 'rushing unbidden' into the divine presence, a more accurate analogy might be of a person apologizing for their tardiness in responding to the divine call!

Suicide as an act of despair

Theologically suicide has been characterized since the time of St Augustine as a damnable sin. This is because it was felt that to kill oneself was to despair of the providence of God. And since the self-chosen death was the person's final action there was no possibility of subsequent repentance. Hence they were deemed to have died faithlessly outside the Church and were denied Christian burial. Happily the Church no longer takes this position, mercifully accepting the likelihood that, in cases of suicide arising from depression, the person's balance of mind was probably disturbed.

It is indeed the case that many suicides are acts of despair. They are particularly tragic when they involve teenagers and people in their early twenties with their whole life before them, who kill themselves during a temporary bout of depression following the failing, or the fear of failing, an exam, or the collapse, or the feared collapse, of a loving relationship. It is very good that Christians today are less judgemental than in the past and seek to do all they can to help young people who are feeling suicidal to come to a more hopeful view of life. However, it is entirely wrong to equate the tragic suicide of a depressed young person with the deliberately chosen death of a person who might well have spent up to a decade fighting a rearguard action against terminal illness.

Why medically assisted suicide should be available to the terminally ill

It is sometimes suggested that there is no need to change the law to allow assisted suicide. Since campaigners for such changes insist that they would only be available to 'competent' persons the question arises of why any truly competent person needs to have a doctor's help to commit suicide. Baroness Finlay argues that

> in the act of suicide the individual is acting autonomously in effecting their wish to die; this does not impinge directly on the autonomy of others, as this is a self-act and does not require another person to be . . . an accessory to the act.[9]

No doubt she is right that some people are well able to commit suicide. When terminal illness follows a long degenerative disease, however, it may well simply become impossible for a person who is by then bedridden and totally dependent on others to acquire the means of self-destruction on their own. Moreover, under the present law, which criminalizes any collaboration or advance knowledge of what is to happen, a suicide must always be a secretive and lonely act. It is also an action that can invalidate certain kinds of life insurance. By contrast, if assisted suicide were legal one could be assured of a swift and painless death, openly say a final farewell to one's nearest and enjoy their support in one's final moments. This would also save one's loved ones from the trauma of the unexpected discovery of one's corpse. It is also important for society as a whole that knowledge about and access to easy means of killing oneself should continue to be relatively restricted. I have already highlighted the tragic suicides of temporarily depressed young people who have actually good grounds for confidence in their futures. In such cases their ignorance of easy means of self-destruction can serve as a useful deterrent, and it is good that this should remain the case.

Could assisted dying take away the opportunity of salvation through deathbed conversion?

According to some traditions within Evangelicalism acceptance of Christ as one's personal saviour was a prerequisite for salvation from hell and everlasting damnation. Hence it was held a matter of great importance to try to obtain a last-minute conversion from the dying person. Samuel Johnson argued that we can never tell the spiritual condition in which a person died for at the very end 'he may in a moment have repented effectually and been accepted by God' like a well-known sinner who died in a fall from a horse of whom it was said:

> Between the stirrup and the ground,
> I mercy sought, I mercy found.[10]

This presupposes a picture of God which raises enormous problems of justice if one can believe that a difference in a person's ultimate destiny for endless millions of years between constant torture on the one hand and eternal bliss on the other can be predicated on so slight a basis. Hospitals and hospices today would not tolerate a chaplaincy service in which the role was seen as frightening the dying into submission to Christian discipleship. Today chaplaincy is seen as ministering to the experienced need of a dying person for spiritual help and support based on the conviction of the universality of God's love.

God as welcoming his prodigal children

The understanding of God presupposed in this book is that picture of God which is most distinctive of Jesus, namely, that God is like a loving father always ready to accept his prodigal children.[11] Clearly on some other understandings of God, suicide would be the ultimate folly. If God were indeed like a heavenly tyrant who would damn a person who had committed suicide to endless punishment on the analogy of a ruler who might sentence to death a deserter in time of war, then euthanasia would be an act of unimaginable folly.

But this view of God is really incompatible with the picture given to us in the teaching of Jesus, and though accepted by some in the past has little support in contemporary Christianity. New Testament criticism has shown fairly conclusively that the analogy of fatherhood was very rare in ancient Judaism prior to Jesus yet this was the way that Jesus constantly referred to God. It is also apparent that Jesus' teaching of the necessity for forgiveness was the most controversial aspect of his thought and is therefore almost certainly distinctive of him. Given this, a Christian may feel confident that God would show the same love and care to someone who had committed suicide as Jesus' followers in today's Samaritan movement seek to show to those who only make the attempt.

Some contemporary Christian perspectives

The Anglican Church has never required its members to believe in hell. This was established in 1864 when it was pointed out that 42 Articles of Religion had been proposed during the Elizabethan settlement but only 39 had been promulgated. An article affirming belief in endless torment was among those omitted. In 1995 the Doctrine Commission went further and in their report *The Mystery of Salvation* declared that belief in hell was incompatible with belief in the love of God.[12]

A comparable perspective of the universality of the love of God in Christ was expressed by Pope John Paul II who unequivocally affirmed in his first encyclical letter *Redemptor Hominis* that 'Every human being without any exception whatever has been redeemed by Christ because Christ is in a way united to the human person – every person without exception even if the individual may not realize this fact.'[13] Given such a perspective the question of an assisted death removing the possibility of last-minute conversion ceases to be an issue.

The sanctity of life

Many people oppose euthanasia and assisted dying because they believe that life is a sacred gift of God to be valued and cherished. Anglican and Catholic bishops affirm together that:

> The whole of humankind is the recipient of God's gift of life. Life is to be received with gratitude and used responsibly. Human beings each have their own distinct identities but these are formed by and take their place within complex networks of relationships. All decisions about individual lives bear upon others with whom we live in community.[14]

The puzzle is why this is supposed to be an argument against assisted dying. A Christian believer may and indeed should rejoice in God's gift of life, value it and treasure it. The Christian believer should also feel a vocation to use life responsibly in the service of others, and always consider the welfare of the community and the network of relationships within which that life is lived. However, precisely because of the high valuation given to that life, the believer may rightly wish to surrender it back to God when it is no longer possible to live life in a creative manner, and when life comes to seem 'burdensome and futile' both to oneself and to the network of relationships within which one lives.

Why assisted suicide is not a repudiation of faith or hope

On past understandings of divine providence it was thought that to accept that one was not going to recover and therefore to request help to die could be thought of as an act of faithless despair, and a proclamation of hopelessness. As such it was seen as an offence against two of the central theological virtues – faith and hope. Here it is important that we confine ourselves to the very limited context of our discussion. We are considering cases where there are no realistic grounds for supposing that recovery is possible, and where, even if some limited remission might occur, it would at best be temporary. There seems no virtue, whether theological or other, in self-delusion. Honest appraisal and a willingness to face reality seem far more appropriate stances. Moreover, it would be a total denial of the most basic Christian beliefs to limit hope to this world. As St Paul puts it, 'If it is for this life only that Christ has given us hope, we of all people are most to be pitied' (1 Cor. 15.19, REB). And if one is speaking of hope in the context of the three theological virtues of faith, hope and love, it is worth reminding ourselves that from a New Testament perspective faith and love 'both spring from that hope stored up for you in heaven' (Col. 1.5, REB). When one speaks of 'The Christian Hope' one is speaking of the historic Christian belief in a life after death. This is the context in which faith and hope are being considered. In a situation where a person's life is clearly drawing to its close, it could be an affirmation of faith, hope and love for a person to choose death voluntarily, entrusting his or her destiny into the loving hands of God. I shall explore this theme in the next chapter.

7

The relevance of the Christian hope to the euthanasia debate

The difference between a Christian and an atheistic world-view

The essential difference between a Christian and a secular world-view can be seen by reflecting on the root meaning of the word 'secular'. This derives from the Latin *saeculum* and connotes that which pertains to the present world or to the present generation. From a secular viewpoint this world is all there is, and death marks the end of our existence. By contrast, from a Christian perspective death is the gateway to eternal life. This should have a profound effect on the way we approach the dying process. If death is not a final terminus, but a junction point from which we move on to a new and fuller life with God, then this calls into question the desirability of straining to keep this mortal life in being if it has become an existence characterized by unbearable suffering with no realistic expectation of relief or recovery.

Why belief in a future life should affect our attitude to euthanasia

Hans Küng points out that:

> Those who trust in God at the same time trust that death is not the end. In the light of the Eternal One, who alone can grant 'deep, deep eternity' the death of mortal life becomes transcended into God's eternal life. As the old prayer for the dead in the eucharist has it, '*Vita mutatur, non tollitur*: life is transformed, not taken away'. So should I be anxiously concerned how short or long this life is finally to be?[1]

Küng argues strongly that if one believes in a life beyond, then when death comes in the fullness of time it should be embraced and accepted, or even, as Hans Küng argues, deliberately chosen, if the alternative is simply prolongation of this life 'under conditions which are no longer commensurate with human dignity'. Küng believes that acceptance of the appropriateness of euthanasia in cases of terminal illness ought to follow from belief that this life is not the end of our existence. As Küng says, 'precisely because I am convinced that another new life is intended for me, as a Christian I see myself given freedom by God to have a say in my dying, a say about the nature and time of my death – in so far as this is granted to me'.[2] To insist that people should put up with suffering that they find unbearable during the dying process seems strange if one takes the Christian hope for life after death seriously.

The centrality of belief in a future life to Christian faith

Belief in life after death is not incidental to Christianity. It is what it came into being to proclaim. According to St Paul the Christian 'good news' (or gospel) is 'first and foremost' that Christ 'was raised to life' and that he had 'appeared' to his disciples after his death and burial. St Paul believed that the whole point of being a Christian was that one now had grounds for belief in a life beyond.

> If the dead are not raised, it follows that Christ was not raised; and if Christ was not raised your faith has nothing to it . . . If it is for this life only that Christ has given us hope, we of all people are most to be pitied . . . But the truth is, Christ was raised to life – the firstfruits of the harvest of the dead. (1 Cor. 15.13–15, 17–20, REB)

Throughout the centuries it is this faith that has been central to Christian identity. It is in no sense a theoretical belief. It is this faith that finds expression in the classic hymns and carols of Easter and in the regular weekly worship of all the Christian Churches. Consider for example the Easter hymn, 'Jesus Lives!'

Jesus lives! Thy terrors now
Can, O Death, no more appal us,
Jesus lives! By this we know
Thou, O grave, canst not enthral us.

It is worth pointing out that almost any Easter hymn could be cited to make the same point. What Easter is about is the believed conquest of death by Jesus' resurrection. If this belief ceased to be held then the hymns would become unsingable.

The communion of the Christian with God

Throughout the Christian centuries, belief in a future life has been at the heart of living faith. One can readily see why this should be so. It is an essential element in the coherence of what Christians claim about God. From the beginning Christianity has believed itself to be the fulfilment of that 'New Covenant' (or New Testament) foretold by Jeremiah and written not on tablets of stone but on the human heart.[3] It is the claim to a direct and personal knowledge of God open to every individual believer. There is the idea that the 'communion of the Christian with God' can be a living reality in human life. The belief is that each individual matters to God and can be known by God. Yet if the believer can truly enter into a relationship with God which God values, and if each individual really matters to the all-powerful and all-loving God, then God will not allow that individual and that relationship to be destroyed by death. If death were simply extinction then this sense of 'the infinite value' of each individual to God would be shown to have been a delusion.

Life after death and the 'problem of evil'

Similarly the Christian conviction that God is love would be equally falsified if death were the final end. The 'problem of evil' has always challenged Christian belief in an all-powerful, all-knowing and all-loving God. The only kind of 'solution' that can begin to address the challenge is one that sees the sufferings of earthly existence as far outweighed by an 'eternal weight of glory beyond all comparison' with it.[4] If, however, every human life simply ends with the sufferings of old age, disease and death there is no way any conceivable 'theodicy' could make sense of that in relation to belief in an all-powerful God of love.

Life after death in doctrine and sacrament

If we turn from belief in God to look at other Christian doctrines we find exactly the same situation. According to the Creeds the incarnation took place 'for us, and for our salvation'. If we have no ultimate salvation it is hard to see what purpose the doctrine serves. The carols of Christmas equally with the hymns of Easter affirm the reality of a life beyond. Consider for example, 'Hark the Herald Angels Sing':

> Mild he lays his glory by,
> Born that man no more may die,
> Born to raise the sons of earth,
> Born to give them second birth.

If we turn to the Christian sacraments we see the same situation. At baptism we become heirs of the kingdom of heaven. At the Eucharist we receive 'the bread of immortality' in the Orthodox liturgy, or the bread of eternal or everlasting life in Anglican and Roman formularies. Likewise reference to God's everlasting kingdom occurs at the most solemn moments of confirmation, marriage, ordination and absolution and if we receive the last rites we are given the Viaticum to nourish the soul for the journey through death.

Although belief in life after death can readily be shown to be an integral part of the historic Christian world-view and necessary for the coherence of Christian beliefs, it is a belief to which many Church leaders and theologians rarely address themselves. I remember being surprised by the realization that I had never been asked to think about the topic in the course of two theological degrees or during the whole of my ordination training. That is why I deliberately chose the topic for my doctorate. It is possible that one reason why both Hans Küng and I have championed the cause of euthanasia from the perspective of Christian theology is because, unlike many of our fellow theologians, both of us have sought to address the question of eternal life.[5]

Contemporary belief in the historicity of the resurrection of Jesus

We should not overstate this relative silence, because there are in fact good grounds on which belief in a future life is being defended today. From the specifically Christian perspective one element in this is renewed confidence in the historicity of the resurrection of Jesus. For many evangelical Christians the grounds for trust in this historicity is that it is the clear teaching of the Gospels. If one treats the Gospel narratives as wholly reliable as in the classic work *Who Moved the Stone?*[6] it is fairly easy to move on to a harmony of the Gospels, in which the obvious solution is that the stone was moved by the angels to enable the emergence of the risen Christ bodily from the tomb.

For liberal Christians, and for those with a more sceptical frame of mind, a stronger case for belief in the historicity of the resurrection is to see it as the best way, or even the only way, of making sense of some indubitable facts about the origins of Christianity. The starting point for such an inquiry is the historical fact that Jesus was crucified, dead and buried. This is one of the few facts about Jesus evidenced from hostile sources. Tacitus, the Roman historian, writing in 110 CE says, 'Christ was crucified by the procurator Pontius Pilate during the reign of Tiberius Caesar'; Celsus, a Greek philosopher writing in the second century, adds his witness to the crucifixion. He sees the degradation of such a death as a powerful argument against faith in Christ. The Jewish Talmud says that Jesus was 'a Rabbi who led Israel astray' and that he was executed on the eve of the Passover.[7]

The second equally certain historical fact is that, shortly after Jesus' death, Christianity came into being as a new religion. The disciples did not simply continue the preaching of Jesus. If they had merely done that, then the Jesus movement might well have continued as a liberal pressure group within Rabbinic Judaism. Instead, the first Christians proclaimed a quite new message based on the resurrection of Jesus, and it was this message of eternal life that came to be distinctive of Christianity. We know that the earliest Christians believed passionately that Jesus had risen from the dead, not only because they were willing to die as witnesses to this but also because they persuaded others to share this belief. Indeed, it is clear that as a matter of history the early Christians believed in life after death with a sense of utter certainty that was recognized both inside and outside the Church as a hallmark of Christian identity. It was their absolute faith in this future hope that enabled the first Christians to embrace martyrdom with composure, and even with enthusiasm, and thereby to convert their persecutors.

There are other historical features associated with the rise of Christianity which require explanation. We know that the process of mourning normally follows a very predictable course with people 'shut in on themselves'.[8] We know that immediately after Jesus' crucifixion this was literally true of his first followers. But suddenly this pattern was broken and they began to proclaim their confidence publicly that he had risen. We know that the earliest Christians made the first day of the week their sacred day in spite of the fact that the earliest Christians were Jews for whom the Sabbath was axiomatically sacrosanct. We know that the early Christians confidently proclaimed that Jesus really was the promised 'Messiah' of Israel: *The Christ*. Indeed we know that this was so integral to their talk about Jesus that the title *Christ* came to function as Jesus' surname within a generation. Yet the Messiahship of one whose life had been simply ended by public execution could never have been subsequently proclaimed to the world if that death had really been the end. Finally, we know that the early Christians rapidly came to think of Jesus as being in some sense God, despite the strict monotheism of the disciples' Jewish heritage. These historical facts require a historically adequate explanation.

The only explanation which seems to me to do justice to all these facts is that Jesus appeared to his disciples and convinced them that he had risen from the dead into a new kind of life. It is therefore with very good reason that the 1938 Commission on Doctrine in the Church of England concluded that the belief that Jesus had risen from the dead was 'an essential part of the Christian message'. However, they also affirmed that belief in the truth of the resurrection is compatible with 'a variety of critical views' about what had actually happened. The reason the Doctrine Commission took this view is that the New Testament evidence presents a variety of interpretations of the nature of the resurrection which is why equally committed Christian scholars come to different conclusions about it.

Why 'reductionist' accounts of the resurrection don't do justice to it

For the resurrection to matter it is important that it was a real historical event and not simply a metaphorical way of asserting the ever-present possibility of making a new start in life. I do not doubt the importance for Christians of believing that fresh beginnings are always possible. That is part of what talk of conversion, forgiveness of sins and rededication are all about. It is the case that the earliest Christians believed that, because of their belief in the resurrection, they were called to a new way of life in the here and now. But this new life was a consequence of prior resurrection belief, and not its cause.

Similarly belief in the resurrection cannot be equated with a decision by the disciples to 'continue Christ's cause'. The reason for saying this is that the earliest Christians didn't 'continue Christ's cause'. They did not focus their attention on the ethical and religious teaching of the historical Jesus as portrayed by the synoptic Gospels. Instead they taught a new message about Christ and his resurrection, and a new and vitalizing hope in life beyond death to which they gave their total commitment. It is this hope that requires a sufficient explanation, and it is the way Christians interpret this that is the clue to how they see the significance of Christ's resurrection for themselves.

Christians differ widely about how the resurrection of Jesus is to be understood and, in particular, whether belief in the empty tomb is central to that belief, or whether the appearances of Jesus to his disciples would have been sufficient to give rise to the Easter faith. Every year scholarly books are published for and against each position. The reason the controversy exists is because New Testament evidence can be cited that is supportive of each position.[9]

But what New Testament scholars and the New Testament itself unite in affirming is that the resurrection of Jesus is central to the Christian hope. Every book of the New Testament was written from that perspective. As a matter of history there is no doubt at all that the resurrection of Jesus gave rise to a wholly new confidence in a life beyond. Adolf Harnack summed up the position thus in the book *What Is Christianity?*

> Whatever may have happened at the grave and in the manner of the appearances, one thing is certain: This grave was the birthplace of the indestructible belief that death is vanquished, that there is life eternal. It is useless to cite Plato; it is useless to point to the Persian religion, and the ideas and the literature of later Judaism. All this would have perished and has perished; but the certainty of the resurrection and of a life eternal which is bound up with the grave in Joseph's garden has not perished, and on the conviction that 'Jesus lives' we still base those hopes of citizenship in an Eternal City which makes our earthly life worth living.[10]

Resurrection in eschatological perspective

A major theme of New Testament scholarship since the time of Schweitzer and Weiss has been a recovery of the apocalyptic emphasis that is believed to have characterized earliest Christianity. This has been taken up into systematic theology by Pannenberg and Moltmann. Pannenberg insists that 'the basis on which the understanding of Jesus rests is always linked to the apocalyptic framework of Jesus' earthly life . . . if this framework is removed then the fundamental basis of faith is lost'.[11] For Moltmann eschatology is 'the key to the whole of Christian faith'.[12] He looks forward to the transformation of the whole world and the whole future. For such writers belief in the empty tomb and bodily resurrection of Jesus is central to faith because what happened to Jesus then will happen to us all at the universal resurrection of the dead at the end of time. This theme is central to Bishop Tom Wright's influential work *The Resurrection of the Son of God* and it is spelt out particularly clearly in Andrew Chester's chapter on 'Eschatology' in *The Blackwell Companion to Modern Theology*. Chester sees the key advantage of this way of thinking in that it does full justice to the biblical stress on the psychosomatic unity of the whole person, and our place within the created order. For Chester the true Christian hope entails 'the recognition that the whole future and all time are set within God's control'.[13] This approach takes absolutely seriously St Paul's thought that 'the universe itself is to be freed from the shackles of mortality and is to enter upon the glorious liberty of the children of God' (Rom. 8.21, REB).

For a Christian who truly shares this hope it should seem absurd to insist on using every possible resource to keep in being a life in the final stages of the dying process. When life has become so shackled to its mortality that the person can no longer do or enjoy anything, and has no earthly future to look forward to, how much the Christian hope has to offer! Rather than linger on for a few more hours or days, how much better to seek assistance to die with dignity, and to commit oneself into the loving hands of God 'in sure and certain hope of the resurrection to eternal life'. In the third century when the Easter hope was a living reality to all Christians, St Athanasius argued that the best evidence for the resurrection of Jesus is the way Christians 'treat death as nothing . . . they go eagerly to meet it . . . rather than remain in this present life'.[14] According to Arthur Droge and James Tabor, before St Augustine changed Christian attitudes to this question (see p. 36), many of the early Christians held the stoic understanding that at the end of life when suffering becomes unbearable and all dignity is being lost, suicide can be 'a noble death'.[15] The beliefs of the early Christians provide an interesting counterbalance to those of their successors today who give priority to the prolongation of life at all costs.

The immortality of the soul and subsequent bodily resurrection

The classic understanding of the Christian hope has two components: belief in the immortality of the soul through death and belief in subsequent bodily resurrection. Both beliefs are affirmed in the New Testament, in the writings of the early Fathers, the theologians of the Middle Ages, the Reformers and in the official teaching of the Roman Catholic Church today. The doctrinal document of the Holy See *On Man's Condition after Death* states:

> The Church affirms that a spiritual element survives and subsists after death, an element endowed with consciousness and will so that the 'human self' subsists, though deprived for the present of the complement of its body. To designate this element the Church uses the word 'soul', the accepted term in the usage of scripture and tradition.[16]

While seeing the immortality of the soul as a necessary bridge for our personhood between this life and the next, however, the Church has always seen the need for some kind of future embodiment as essential for a truly personal existence. In the old Roman Creed this was seen as a literal resurrection of 'this flesh' and in the Apostles' Creed of 'the flesh'. However, 'bodily resurrection' does not have to be interpreted this way even if this was how it was interpreted in the second century.[17] In the sixteenth century Archbishop Cranmer altered 'resurrection of the flesh' to 'resurrection of the body'. Cranmer was well aware that the Latin word *carnis* meant 'flesh', but though he himself might have been willing to affirm such a belief he felt that 'resurrection of the body' was more in tune with the language of the New Testament. St Paul believed that our 'inner nature' will have 'a new body put on over it'[18] and in 1 Corinthians 15 he drew a succession of vivid distinctions between earthly and heavenly bodies. This view was spelt out more fully in the Archbishops' Commission on Doctrine in 1938:

> We ought to reject quite frankly the literalistic belief in a future resuscitation of the actual physical frame which is laid in the tomb . . . none the less . . . in the life of the world to come the soul or spirit will still have its appropriate organ of expression and activity, which is one with the body of earthly life in the sense that it bears the same relation to the same spiritual entity. What is important when one is speaking of the identity of any person's 'body' is not its psycho-physical constitution, but its relation to that person.[19]

In 1995 the Doctrine Commission put this slightly differently. They argued that the 'essence of humanity is certainly not the matter of the body, for that is continuously changing . . . What provides continuity and unity through that flux of change is not material but [in a vague but suggestive phrase] the vastly complex information-bearing pattern in which that material is organized. That pattern can surely be considered the carrier of memories and of personality.'[20] What happens at death according to this theory is that 'Death dissolves the embodiment of that pattern, but the person whose pattern that is, is "remembered" by God, who in love holds that unique being in his care.' However, there must at some point be a 'fuller realization of God's purpose for us all'. This will come with 'the resurrection of the body'. But 'it is not to be supposed that the material of the resurrected body is the same as that of the old'.[21]

The credibility of life after death in a Christian understanding of reality

Is such a hope credible today? Such a question needs to be re-expressed: 'Credible to whom?' All rational believing reflects the overall world-view of the believer. It seems to me that belief in the immortality of the soul followed by resurrection of the body (however understood) depends for its coherence on believing that it is something that God could and would wish to bring about. Austin Farrer, John Hick and I have argued elsewhere that since modern physics accepts the possibility of plural spaces in no relationship with one another, it would be logically possible for heaven to exist in another space (or perhaps better 'another dimension of being') in no relationship with our own universe.[22] Resurrection belief is therefore a possibility, and it would tie in with the insight of that section of St Paul's discussion of resurrection life in 1 Corinthians 15 in which he affirms both the reality of bodily resurrection and also its radical difference from our life in the here and now. We shall also see below that there is now evidence that the first stage of the process, namely, the immortality of the soul, can be supported both by empirical evidence and philosophical reasoning. Hence I suggest that belief in life after death is a reasonable and indeed a necessary belief for anyone who genuinely believes in the claims of the Christian faith about God and the unique importance of each individual person to God. Since Christians engaged in euthanasia debates always do affirm their commitment to the sanctity and importance of each individual to God they need to see the implications of taking account of the dimension of life after death. I claim that, once this belief is fully brought into the picture, it is reasonable for a Christian to welcome death as bringing to an end the sufferings of terminal illness. It is tragic that this dimension is so missing from contemporary Christianity that the verse of St Francis of Assisi about death is asterisked for omission in most contemporary hymn books:

> And thou most kind and gentle death
> Waiting to hush our latest breath
> O praise Him, Alleluia
> Thou bringest home the child of God,
> And Christ our Lord this way hast trod
> O praise Him, O praise Him, Alleluia alleluia, alleluia.

Near-death experiences

As a result of the latest medical advances it has become increasingly possible to resuscitate people from apparent death. What we find is that something like 10 per cent of people who have undergone a cardiac arrest report a series of experiences while in this condition. They claim that after their hearts had stopped beating and their lungs stopped breathing 'they' went out of their bodies. They describe looking down and remembering the resuscitation procedures and they talk of life-review, telepathic meetings and enhanced religious awareness.

Consultant neurophysiologist Dr Peter Fenwick claims that recent studies of near-death experiences in hospital contexts have shown that such experiences take place in the absence of any recordable brain activity.[23] The best-known such case is that of Pam Reynolds who underwent a life-threatening operation to remove an aneurysm from her brain. To prevent blood circulating around her head during the operation her heart was stopped, her body temperature was lowered, and she was for all practical purposes temporarily dead with no measurable brain function.

Nevertheless after the operation she correctly described what had happened during it to the amazement of the doctors involved. Most evidentially because she was a professional musician she was able to tell the doctors that the drill that opened up her skull vibrated as a natural D. This instrument had not been used until she was totally unconscious and none of the doctors had a clue about the musical note at which the drill vibrated. But it turned out that she was right.[24]

The phenomena of correct observations made while the person was deeply unconscious is one of the most convincing aspects of the near-death experience. These phenomena happen. This is recognized even by the most sceptical of critics, Dr Susan Blackmore. She accepts that 'there is no doubt that people describe reasonably accurately events that have occurred around them during their near-death experience'. However, she suggests that these observations can be explained naturalistically as a combination of 'prior knowledge, fantasy, and lucky guesses and the remaining operating senses of hearing and touch'.[25] This hypothesis was tested by Dr Penny Sartori, a staff nurse in an intensive therapy unit. She found, as others have, that people who have a near-death experience do indeed describe reasonably accurately how they were resuscitated. But she decided additionally to ask people who had been resuscitated without having a near-death experience if they also could describe how they were resuscitated. They could not do so. Their attempts were hopelessly wrong.[26] So it seems that the factors Dr Blackmore suggested as explaining the observations are not enough. People need additionally to have a near-death experience. The fact that those who have had a near-death experience do get the observations correct may be because 'they' really were out-of-their-bodies and actually did observe themselves from above in the way they claimed to do.

It is important that further research should check these findings because if, even for only a few seconds near the point of death, people can really get out of their bodies and observe correctly from a different vantage point then brain and mind are not identical and the immortality of the soul is a possibility. They certainly change the intellectual climate in relation to belief in a future life. For example, although the famous twentieth-century atheist philosopher Antony Flew continues to 'hope and believe' there is no afterlife, he accepts that 'this evidence [about near-death experiences] certainly weakens if it does not completely refute my arguments against doctrines of a future life'.[27] Likewise the Australian sociologist Allan Kellehear believes that the most important impact of near-death experiences is that they have 'put the idea of survival of death back on the religious agenda'.[28]

Is dualism compatible with neurology?

The claim that one can go out of one's body implies a belief in dualism. Most philosophers and theologians today reject soul–body dualism because of all that modern science has shown us about the intimate relationship that exists between all our thinking, feeling and willing and some quite specific brain states. However, these facts can be explained equally well by a doctrine of mind–brain interaction. John Hick takes for granted everything that modern genetics and neurophysiology say about the origins of our individuality and hence rejects the idea of a soul being inserted into a developing foetus. The reality of human freedom and spirituality also has to be taken into account, however, and in this context what matters is not origins but ends. Hence Hick believes that it remains possible to see the soul as a real but emergent property and in fact to take literally Keats's insight that this life is a 'vale of soul-making'. According to Hick, 'Distinctive human mentality and spirituality emerges in accordance with the divine purpose in complex bodily organisms. But once it has emerged it is the vehicle, according to Christian faith, of a continuing creative activity only the beginnings of which have so far taken place.'[29]

Similar positions are taken by both Richard Swinburne and Keith Ward. According to Swinburne, dualism is 'inescapable' if we are really to explain human existence and experience.[30] First, he points out that 'though the mental life of thought, sensation and purpose may be caused by physico-chemical events in the brain, it is quite different from those events'. Second, he draws attention to the fact that 'conscious experiences are causally efficacious. Our thoughts and feelings are not just phenomena caused by goings-on in the brain; they cause other thoughts and feelings and they make a difference to the agent's behaviour.' Third, he suggests that 'though a human soul has a structure and character which is formed in part through the brain to which it is connected . . . [it] acquires some independence of that brain'.[31] Keith Ward adopts the same position: 'Of course the soul depends on the brain . . . but the soul need not always depend on the brain, any more than a man need always depend on the womb which supported his life before birth.'[32]

On this hypothesis the soul is an emergent property that comes into existence in the course of life. Throughout life it interacts with the body but in principle it is separable from it and at death separation occurs. This hypothesis would appear to be not only logically possible but also supported by the latest research into near-death experiences.

If life after death is believed in, it ought to affect our thinking on euthanasia

What I have argued for in this chapter is that belief in life after death is not only a belief that is crucial for the coherence of Christianity, it is also a belief for which there is evidence. The evidence may not be sufficient to persuade an outsider to believe in life after death. But it is adequate to establish the reasonable-ness of a committed Christian holding such a belief. What I claim is that the evidence from near-death experiences coupled with the historical evidence for the resurrection of Jesus and the logical possibility either of re-creation at the end of history or re-embodiment in another dimension of being all show that it is possible to spell out the Christian hope in ways that are reason-able. They are reasonable in the sense that we can conceive their possibility without having to contradict other well-established beliefs that we may have about the nature of reality, and reason-able also in the sense that they are integral to and constitutive of an overall Christian world-view.

In these circumstances it seems to me entirely appropriate that a Christian who believes in life after death should have that belief respected. If in the final stages of terminal illness such a Christian should conclude that he or she no longer wishes to continue to suffer unbearably in this life, but would rather move on to the next, then this choice should be respected. And if assistance to die is requested it would be good if it were legal for this choice to be as permissible as any other request for a last favour from a dying person.

8

Euthanasia and the problem of suffering

Why suffering is a central theme in the debate

Most advocates of euthanasia do so on the grounds that if a person is suffering unbearably in the final stages of a terminal illness, it should be possible to offer them the alternative of a swift and painless death. Opponents of euthanasia also see this issue as crucial, but from two very different angles. From the perspective of Christian theology the suffering is seen by some as having value for our spiritual and personal growth, and should therefore be accepted as part of what it means for us to be fully human. From this point of view euthanasia is resisted as denying us an important element in our full human experience. From the perspective of palliative care, however, euthanasia is opposed for the entirely different reason that, according to many palliative care spokespersons, suffering can be so alleviated by good palliative care that it ought no longer to be seen as grounds for legalizing euthanasia.

The value of redemptive suffering

From the beginning of Christianity the passion of Christ has been seen as an event of the utmost importance. Indeed we may go further back and see Christianity as appropriating to its understanding of Christ's death the spiritual insights of the 'suffering servant' passages of Second Isaiah:

> He was despised and rejected by men;
> a man of sorrows, and acquainted with grief . . .
> Surely he has borne our griefs and carried our sorrows; . . .
> But he was wounded for our transgressions,

83

> he was bruised for our iniquities;
> upon him was the chastisement that made us whole.
>
> (Isa. 53.3–5)

It has always been a central theme of traditional Christian witness that the pain that Christ endured on the cross was good, so that even today we describe the anniversary of his crucifixion as 'Good Friday'. The value of redemptive suffering is not simply to be seen in the death of Christ, however; rather it is sometimes presented in Roman Catholic theology as the vocation of Christians to share in the redemptive suffering of Christ on the cross. St Paul rejoiced in his own suffering because it meant that in his flesh he could help to 'complete what is lacking in Christ's afflictions' (Col. 1.24). On this view what the dying Christian is called to do is to unite his or her sufferings with the sufferings of Christ and to offer them up to God. To opt out of the sufferings of terminal illness would be to repudiate the opportunities such suffering provides for our spiritual growth.

This way of thinking is central to Pope John Paul II's *Declaration on Euthanasia* where we read that:

> Suffering, especially in the final moments of life, has a special place in God's plan of salvation. It is a sharing in the passion of Christ and unites the person with the redemptive sacrifice which Christ offered in obedience to the Father's will. It is not surprising, then, that some Christians desire painkillers only in moderation so that they can deliberately accept at least part of their suffering and thus consciously unite themselves with the crucified Christ.[1]

Pope John Paul II sought to embody these convictions through his own embrace of the dying process. His decision not to retire early in the face of his mortal disease, but to live out his dying in the public eye testifies to his conviction of the need to draw attention to this long-established way of Christian thinking. However, it seems to me that this way of thinking should not be used as an argument to prevent euthanasia being available for people who do not share the Pope's understanding of the Christian faith or who do not wish to take upon themselves this *vocation* of suffering.

I am very conscious of how deeply the kind of argument Pope John Paul II used is rooted in much of the Christian tradition. It will be clear to readers that my father's last poem, 'Questioning', which I quote in full in my dedication of this book to him, shows how he struggled to affirm a commitment to this belief despite the agonies through which he went. Reading and rereading his poem, and thinking back to the last months of his life, I cannot help thinking that his suffering was made worse by his belief in a vocational duty to embrace suffering and to find 'meaning' in it. What he most wanted was to die and entrust himself into the hands of God. Instead he had to choose between a life of mental alertness but ever present pain, or a pain-free existence in a heroin-induced dream world. A priest of his generation and his belief system would not have chosen an assisted death, even if that had been available. But I cannot help but think that it would have been so much better for him if both the law of the land and the teaching of the Church could have enabled him to lay down his life with dignity at the time of his choosing.

Some theological problems with belief in redemptive suffering

For many Christians today the idea that we are called to participate in the sufferings of Christ is open to serious objection. For traditional evangelical Protestantism the grounds for their objection are expressed clearly in the prayer of consecration in the 1662 Prayer Book. This states that 'by his one oblation of himself once offered' Christ 'made . . . a full, perfect, and sufficient sacrifice, oblation, and satisfaction, for the sins of the whole world'. From such a perspective there is no possibility of our suffering 'making up what was lacking' in Christ's suffering as if that was in any way insufficient for salvation.

Liberal Christians oppose the idea from a very different perspective. They think that the idea that Christ's death was 'a sacrifice by which God was placated' is a horrific notion even though taught by such giants of the faith as Aquinas, Luther and Calvin.[2] According to F. D. Maurice the idea of Christ's dying to appease the wrath of God is a denial of the doctrine of the incarnation:

'We must not dare to speak of Christ changing that Will which he took flesh and died to fulfil.'[3] From the perspective of historical New Testament studies Jesus was put to death because he offended influential religious leaders of his day by teaching the limitless forgiveness of God, and for teaching that religious laws were made for the benefit of human beings, not human beings for the benefit of religious laws.[4] Jesus literally died 'for the forgiveness of sins' because if one explores the Gospel accounts of where his teaching was perceived to be most controversial it was precisely on that issue that he was most strongly opposed. Jesus died because he was faithful to the good news he felt called to teach. He brought at-one-ment with God by breaking down the idea that a wrathful God was always keeping tabs on us. Instead he taught that God is most like a loving father always rushing to welcome back and to forgive his prodigal children.[5] The good news of Christianity is not to be seen in the tragic death of Christ but in his vindication by God through his resurrection from the dead. For the first ten centuries Christian iconography focused on the empty cross as the symbol of Jesus' resurrection rather than on the crucifix, as the emblem of his passion. If we truly believe in the central message of Jesus Christ that 'God is love', it cannot be the case that God requires us to suffer needlessly after our work is done and our lives have come to their natural end.

Can suffering communicate dignity and assurance?

The idea that faith should enable us to experience suffering in a positive manner was an important element in the Archbishop of Canterbury's speech opposing Lord Joffe's Assisted Dying Bill.

> All religious believers hold that there is no stage of human life, and no level of human experience, that is intrinsically incapable of being lived through in some kind of trust and hope. They would say that to suggest otherwise is to limit the possibility of faithful and hopeful lives to those who are in charge of their circumstances or who enjoy a measure of control and success. Believers hold that even experiences of pain and helplessness can be passed through in a way that is meaningful and that communicates dignity and assurance.[6]

The Archbishop is right that 'experiences of pain and helplessness *can* be passed through in a way that is meaningful and that communicates dignity and assurance'. The difficulty is, however, that that is not the way that most people respond to suffering. The more general human experience of suffering is that however 'bravely borne' it is rarely ennobling, and is more likely to lead to the collapse of faith than to its enhancement.

This is particularly true in the case of people facing the long-drawn-out process of dying today. Dr Julia Lawton in her observation of 'patients' experience of palliative care' came across no one whose faith had been strengthened by it. On the contrary, 'the very distressing ways in which some patients deteriorated and rotted away within the hospice, prompted a small, but significant minority of hitherto religious patients to question their faith and sometimes to abandon it altogether'.[7] Michael Young and Lesley Cullen in their survey of people's ideas of a good death also show how a person can 'be robbed of faith' by the 'experiences of their final weeks'.[8]

If suffering is good why do we use painkillers?

A further objection to the idea that suffering is good for us is that this notion ought not to be used as an argument against euthanasia unless one were prepared to accept the other implication of this hypothesis and refrain from administering painkilling drugs. It is clear that Pope John Paul II accepted this implication. He urged that painkillers should only be used in moderation so that people can have the experience of terminal suffering. My father also sought to follow that route as far as he was able, yet few today take that line. Almost everyone concerned with dying people accepts the duty and responsibility to do everything in their power to minimize the discomfort of the terminally ill. This was also a biblical good, as commended in the proverbial injunction to 'Give strong drink to him who is perishing' (Prov. 31.6). We can now do better than that, and the goal of palliative medicine is to search for a balance of medication at precisely the right dosage to control all pain. If suffering were genuinely believed to be good this is not the policy that would be followed.

The moral value of bravery

In former ages there was very little that could be done to reduce suffering. The painkillers we routinely use like aspirin, paracetamol and ibuprofen did not exist until the present century. The opiates used in modern medicine were not readily available in the Western world before their first use and abuse as laudanum in the early nineteenth century. Prior to these there was nothing that could be done but to grit one's teeth or seek the oblivion of alcohol. Stoicism in the face of pain was, under such circumstances, a real virtue because it spared one's loved ones a full knowledge of what one was going through. Traditional theology made a virtue out of necessity in suggesting that we seek to find meaning in and through suffering.

Taking up the cross and following Christ

In Luke 14.27 Jesus said that 'whoever does not bear his own cross and come after me cannot be my disciple'. From the beginning Christians have recognized that a willingness to embrace suffering for the sake of the gospel is part of what following Christ means. In the early centuries of Christianity the blood of the martyrs was literally the seed of the Church.[9] Christianity became a world-wide religion only through the willingness of countless missionaries to face disease and death in foreign climes across the world. In the twentieth century the martyred theologian Dietrich Bonhoeffer spelt out that the cost of discipleship for the 'Confessing Church' entailed a willingness to risk everything for the sake of opposing the Nazi regime.[10] In the former Soviet Union, in China during the 'cultural revolution', in South Korea during the Japanese occupation and the Communist invasion, and in some areas of Africa today the survival of Christianity depended on faithful Christians witnessing to the death for the sake of the gospel.

But taking up the cross does not mean that Christians are under an obligation to take on unnecessary suffering. There have been periods in the past when asceticism has been much prized but Christians today do not feel it integral to their discipleship.

Masochism is not normally regarded as a virtue, and contemporary Christianity no longer admires the wearing of hair shirts or self-flagellation. In the same way I suggest it should no longer be seen as a virtue to endure the pains of death when modern medication can enable us to be released from them.

The analogy between the pains of death and the pains of birth

If we turn to a potential parallel with the pains of death, and that is to the pains of childbirth, it is significant that today effective pain relief is seen as every woman's right. This was not always so. When analgesics were first introduced in the form of chloroform in childbirth, their use was strongly opposed by much Christian opinion. It was argued that according to the Bible women 'in pain . . . shall bring forth children'.[11] Their suffering was explicitly seen as an integral part of God's plan of salvation, just as John Paul II continued to see the pains of death as part of God's plan. But few Christians think that way today. Women in Britain are generally appreciative that Queen Victoria insisted on her right to anaesthesia in childbirth, thereby making this an acceptable choice for them as well. This does not exclude the possibility of an individual woman deciding for herself that she will have an entirely natural birth so that she can fully experience her child's arrival. Indeed she has that right. I suggest that since at least as many people today believe in the desirability of pain-free death as of pain-free birth the law should reflect their wishes in both situations while accepting that those who feel they have a vocation to suffer can experience the full process of dying.

John Hick's soul-making theodicy and the necessity of suffering

The starting point for John Hick's attempt to justify the goodness of God in the face of the suffering we experience in the world comes from a letter of the dying poet John Keats to his brother and sister in 1819. Keats writes:

> Do you not see how necessary a world of pain and troubles is to
> school an intelligence and make it a Soul . . . Call the world if you
> please 'the vale of soul-making'.[12]

Does this imply that suffering is a necessary part of Hick's philosophy of religion? I think not. Hick's theodicy is that we shape
our personhood by the way we engage with the responsibilities
and duties we face in a world where what we do, or fail to do,
has consequences. A real objective physical world, governed by
regular physical laws, provides an environment more suited to the
development of responsible agents than would an environment
in which divine intervention saved humanity from the consequences of its folly. The existence of suffering is an inevitable
concomitant of life in such a world. But it is no part of Hick's
theodicy to suggest that suffering in itself is either ennobling or
character-forming. Hick believes there is strong evidence against
so simplistic a view. He is in fact a member of Dignity in Dying
and his thesis assumes the reality of a future life. It is there that
he sees the resolution of the problems of suffering inherent in our
present existence. There is nothing in Hick's theodicy, correctly
understood, to suggest that we should voluntarily endure any
physical suffering from which we have the means to deliver ourselves.[13] It may also be noted that Keats himself would have
welcomed the possibility of an assisted death as was realized by
Baroness Warnock and Elisabeth Macdonald in choosing their
book's title, *Easeful Death*, from Keats's 'Ode to a Nightingale':

> Darkling I listen; and, for many a time
>   I have been half in love with easeful Death,
> Call'd him soft names in many a musèd rhyme,
>   To take into the air my quiet breath;
> Now more than ever seems it rich to die,
>   To cease upon the midnight with no pain[.]

Is suffering a valid reason for euthanasia?

Lord Joffe's primary motivation for introducing his Assisted Dying
Bill was his belief that 'Some terminally-ill patients suffer terrible
deaths and the Bill is about preventing unnecessary suffering.'[14]

His Bill was opposed most strongly by specialists in palliative medicine who argued that modern advances in palliative care have so improved the care of the dying that instances of irreversible, protracted and unbearable suffering ought to be extremely rare. Baroness Finlay believes a 'patient's request for euthanasia is a cry for help' and when that help has been given and symptom control achieved 'the experience of those working in hospices is that requests for euthanasia do not persist'.[15] I rejoice in such developments, and very much wish that the spread of palliative medicine and hospice care would enable more people to die in dignity and peace without the need to resort to euthanasia. But this does not weaken the case for allowing euthanasia in those cases where painful suffering remains inescapably present. It is also abundantly clear from Dr Julia Lawton's study of patients' experiences of palliative care that some hospice patients do persistently and continuously beg for assistance to die.

The persistence of pain

The distinguished Yale physician Sherwin Nuland in his book *How We Die* documents just how devastating the process of dying can be. Nuland believes that we do people a grave disservice if we lead them to believe that they can expect to die with dignity, or that their suffering can always be alleviated. He believes that the trauma of dying for both patient and family has been greatly intensified in recent years because they have been misled into believing that modern medication can control their suffering. Nuland believes the odds are overwhelmingly against this.[16] It seems that Nuland is right about the odds. Carmen Dupont, the Policy and Information Officer for Dignity in Dying cites a survey published in the *Pharmaceutical Journal* in 2007 which found that between 60 per cent and 90 per cent of patients in palliative care do not currently receive adequate pain relief.[17] A report of the Nuffield Trust on the care of the dying also says that 'too often patients' last weeks, days and hours of life are spent in avoidable pain, discomfort and confusion'.[18] This ought not to happen in that, according to Illora Finlay, 95 per cent of pain in terminal illness can and should be controlled.[19] Nigel Biggar goes further and argues that actually 'there is no such thing as pain that cannot be relieved in so far as permanent sedation can always be used as a last resort'.[20]

Suffering is much wider than pain

Dignity in Dying recognizes that pain can and should normally be controlled but they point out that suffering is much wider than pain. Carmen Dupont, their Policy and Information Officer, cites surveys that show that terminal breathlessness is very difficult to treat in cancer patients and that up to 70 per cent of such patients will suffer from this.[21] She also points out that

> Despite the constant progress in palliative care and the great work done by nurses and doctors on a daily basis, some other symptoms can sometimes be difficult to manage, for example, bedsores, loss of appetite, nausea, episodes of lowered consciousness, confusion/delirium and incontinence. These symptoms can prove to be very distressing for patients.[22]

An even more pessimistic picture is spelt out graphically by the Cambridge researcher in cell death in the brain, heart, and cancer, Guy Brown, in his work, *The Living End*.[23] It seems that even though pain can normally be controlled, nothing can lessen the slow disintegration of our personhood that many of us will experience from one or other degenerative disease. Reading Brown's chapters on 'Falling apart' and 'Losing one's marbles' brings home just how traumatic and prolonged the process of dying from cancer, gradual heart failure, or Alzheimer's disease can actually be.

Is sedation the answer?

We have already noted Nigel Biggar's claim that all pain and suffering can be eliminated by making full use of permanent sedation as a last resort. Mary Warnock and Elisabeth Macdonald show that the use of sedation does not shorten life but does eliminate suffering and that, in the specialist palliative unit they looked at, 48 per cent of patients were sedated for the last 48 hours of life, and some for much longer periods before death.[24] However, there is a question of whether the fairly routine application of the 'last

resort' of permanent sedation, sufficient to obliterate all awareness of any pain, is morally distinguishable from euthanasia. In
both cases the patient's consciousness ceases, and the expression
'terminal sedation' is probably a more accurate description of the
patient's condition.

The prevalence of continuous sedation raises a theological
problem about the meaning of such lives. If our experiences in
this life are seen theologically as a means of growth and development it is hard to see that keeping life in being in a situation of
constant medication helps a Christian understanding of what life
is for. Many who value above all their sentience and rationality
would rather endure pain than spend their final days in a dream-
world of narcotic illusion. Such people might well wish to have
their life ended while they were still in control of their faculties,
rather than to continue for a few months longer as helpless
dependants on opiates at the end of life. This may be particularly
true of those most committed to Christian values who may well
have fought against a drug culture throughout their lives and have
no wish to succumb to it in their last weeks.

How far suffering can be palliated

To focus on pain rather than the other harbingers of approach-
ing death is a mistake. What most people find 'unbearable' in their
terminal illness is not pain, but rather the loss of their independence, their dignity, their prospects for enjoying life and their ability to control their bodily functions. Baroness Finlay shows that
a sympathetic and thoughtful approach on the part of the palliative team can do much to help even here. For example, good nursing care will seek to convey total acceptance of the dying person's
dignity even when this is threatened by episodes of urinary or
faecal incontinence. In such contexts it would be important to
talk of the urine 'coming away' rather than of the patient 'wetting
themselves'.[25] Likewise, when a person is incapable of absorbing
nourishment in the normal way it might be preferable to feed
them through a feeding tube direct to the stomach rather than
through a nasogastric tube through the nose to the stomach. Giving
it directly to the stomach could enable a terminally ill cancer

sufferer to go out to a pub to see his friends once more, swill some beer around his mouth to get the taste of the beer, and then pour the rest through a funnel into the stomach tube to enable him to feel the effects of the alcohol on his brain.[26]

I remember in the discussions leading up to the *Facing Death* book Baroness Finlay gave another example. This was the case of a woman whose face had already been so eaten away by cancer that she could not bring herself to go out in public. In her case, Baroness Finlay suggested that she dress as if she were a devout Muslim with a veil shielding her face from view. This suggestion found welcome acceptance and the woman was no longer completely imprisoned in her home during her final illness.

These examples of good palliative care show how careful thought for the wellbeing of the individual can make a real difference to them. But of necessity such actions can only 'palliate' an underlying condition which some would continue to find intolerable. For me such examples bring home the ghastliness of the dying process, rather than give me comfort about how suffering can be reduced by such procedures.

Spirituality and palliative care

Dr Cicely Saunders founded the first modern hospice, St Christopher's, in London in 1967. She sought to unite spirituality and medicine in the pastoral care of the terminally ill. She argued that each individual should be given adequate and balanced pain relief and helped to live life to the full until they died. Her work inspired the growth of the hospice movement throughout Britain. Her ideals have deeply influenced the Churches' understanding of what palliative care can achieve. Over the years, talks about St Christopher's Hospice have been an important part of the ministerial formation of the clergy. I remember how moved I was by Dr Saunders's presentation at my own theological college. The ideal she painted of how the terminally ill should be looked after, and her presentation of palliative care as alternative to, rather than complementary to, euthanasia has been deeply influential in shaping church opposition to assisting dying.

The loss of the spiritual dimension in palliative care

Although the hospice movement has continued to spread and its work has influenced the spread of good palliative care into hospitals and nursing homes it has been particularly hard to keep alive the spiritual ideals which initially shaped the movement. Julia Lawton cites ten research studies each of which document 'a shift in emphasis away from the spiritual, emotional and social care of dying patients to a concentration upon their physical symptoms'.[27] As Tony Walter explains, 'It is easier to demonstrate effective pain control, high bed occupancy and financial cost per patient than to demonstrate real attentiveness to patients' wishes.'[28]

Hospices have also suffered from their very success in providing the best palliative care in that they have come under increasing pressure to accept patients with the worst medical symptoms. Unfortunately such patients also have the least capacity to prepare psychologically or spiritually for death.[29]

Patients' experiences of palliative care and the bodily realities of the dying process

The fullest account of the present situation, based on her own observed experiences of patients, and on an exhaustive literature survey is that provided by Dr Julia Lawton, a senior research fellow in health behaviour and change, in the University of Edinburgh. Before she began her research she read many accounts written by hospice professionals with their reassuring message that with 'compassionate care and effective methods of pain control it is possible to preserve the dignity of patients right up to the point of death'. She notes that 'a somewhat romanticised conception of dying patients resting comfortably in bed, mentally alert, calm and re-assured is all too prevalent within this literature'.[30] Her high expectations of what she would find in hospices were partly confirmed in that they 'often successfully alleviate pain'.[31] She also comments:

> I saw nothing but excellent standards of care . . . Staff and volunteers . . . display a warmth, humanity and professionalism which I

found quite remarkable. What I was unprepared for was somewhat different: it was the visible signs of bodily decay; the stench of incontinence; the lethargy and despondency of the patient . . . the burnout and exhaustion experienced by their families and friends . . . [and] the protracted period of suffering that can occur prior to death.[32]

Her book *The Dying Process* focuses on what she calls 'the bodily realities of dying'.[33] She spells out in detail what it can be like for a patient to suffer total incontinence, constant vomiting, and the eating away of flesh by the growth of cancers. She notes how patients feel the humiliation of total dependency on others and the distress of being unable to engage in meaningful relationships with others. In many cases hospice patients exhibit the kind of 'switching off' noted in Holocaust victims, 'overwhelmed by physical helplessness and despair'. In this situation some patients repeatedly asked for help to die. Others sought total withdrawal through requesting heavy sedation.[34]

Lawton compared hospice patients with other terminally ill patients and notes that studies have found that 'patients who receive hospice care are more likely than other patients with similar physical and mental conditions to express the view that it would have been better if they had died earlier'.[35] She believes that 'in highlighting the bodily realities of dying [her] study raises the question of whether, in the end, "a dignified death" is something we can realistically hope for let alone expect'.[36] Her pessimism about the likelihood of our dying with the dignity we hope for under present conditions would seem confirmed by a poll conducted by the Royal College of Nursing which found that 81 per cent of nurses 'sometimes or often left work feeling distressed or upset because they could not give patients the kind of dignified care that they should'.[37]

End-of-life concerns

In 2005 a report by the Department of Human Services in Oregon analysed the end-of-life concerns of all Oregonians who had actually obtained a medically assisted death between 1998 and 2004.[38] Their concerns were:

- losing autonomy: 87 per cent
- less able to engage in activities making life enjoyable: 84 per cent
- loss of dignity: 80 per cent
- losing control of bodily functions: 59 per cent
- burden on family, friends/caregivers: 36 per cent
- inadequate pain control or concern about it: 22 per cent
- financial implications of treatment: 3 per cent.

It is important that the above list reflects multiple answers. It would be a mistake, for example, to suggest that it shows that 36 per cent chose an assisted death because they were worried about being a burden to others. Such worries were always associated with the far more significant feeling of 'loss of autonomy'. The terminally ill lose their autonomy because as they decline into death virtually everything has to be done for them by other people. The more sensitive among the dying are additionally aware that this places a burden on others but that is never a major factor in their decision, though perhaps from a Christian perspective it should be! However, what is clear from the above list is that what people actually find so unbearable that they seek release in death is the loss of their autonomy, enjoyment and dignity. No one who obtained assistance to die actually suffered from uncontrolled pain, even though one in five were scared that that might one day happen to them.[39]

The deepest fears of the terminally ill

It is often argued that Christians should oppose euthanasia on the grounds that if assisted suicide were legalized this would put pressure on the terminally ill, the old and the infirm to ask for it. But this fear of what might happen if euthanasia were to be legalized is as nothing compared with the far greater fears the elderly have at present through the absence of a euthanasia law. This is the fear that they will be forced to suffer the agony of a long-drawn-out battle against death which doctors will fight over the battlefield of their bodies, in defiance of their wishes.

In their conversations with Londoners, Michael Young and Lesley Cullen found that

> A stock nightmare of modern times is of doctors in the posses-sion of the power to keep us alive when our bodies are at least partly dead, trussed up with tubes to put in and draw out fluids and to keep the semblance of life going with the aid of life support machines of frightening ingenuity. The prospect of being kept alive against one's will (or when one is not in a position to express it) is more frightening than the prospect of being killed.[40]

Patrick Nowell Smith, sometime president of the World Federa-tion of Right to Die Societies shows what a high proportion of the population share these sorts of fears.[41] According to Hans Küng it is the present situation, where people are denied assistance to die, that really puts pressure on the terminally ill. He claims that very often terminally ill people are 'exposed to intolerable suffer-ing at the very point when their helplessness is at its greatest'. He urges that 'it is precisely the most vulnerable who should be allowed the means to ensure that their lives are not dragged out endlessly'. Küng believes that if assisted suicide were allowed it would enable people to die, not in lonely isolation, but 'supported by true friends and with the help of an understanding doctor, in composure and confidence, in gratitude and in tranquil expecta-tion'.[42] Whether or not this is what assisted dying can really give we must leave to the next chapter.

9

End-of-life decision-making in the Netherlands, Oregon and Britain

We saw in Chapter 5 that the main ground for opposition to allowing assisted dying for people suffering unbearably in the final stages of terminal illness is a fear of its possible consequences in changing the moral climate. It is suggested that if voluntary euthanasia were to be allowed for the mentally competent, there would inevitably be pressure for it to be extended to the mentally incompetent; and that there would also be a risk of a slide from voluntary euthanasia to involuntary euthanasia. It is claimed that any such act would put at risk the security of the chronically sick, the disabled, the elderly, the poor and the uneducated, who might feel pressurized into asking for euthanasia. It is also suggested that to allow euthanasia could undermine the trust between doctor and patient.

Are these fears justified? One way of answering such questions is to look at the actual experience of euthanasia in countries where it is allowed, particularly in the Netherlands, where euthanasia has been openly practised since the early seventies, and in the US State of Oregon where assisted dying has been legal since 1997. In making this examination we must also be aware that in countries where neither euthanasia nor assisted dying are permitted, it remains the case that the complexities of modern medicine require doctors to make end-of-life decisions on behalf of their patients and that the distinction between the two situations is not always clear.

Voluntary euthanasia in the Netherlands

Mary Warnock points out that euthanasia has only been legal in the Netherlands since 2002 with the coming into force of the Termination of Life on Request and Assisted Suicide (Review Procedures) Act of 2001, which 'regularized and legitimized the situation of doctors'.[1] Prior to that the situation was that, though euthanasia was illegal, a succession of court cases in the early seventies acquitted doctors of any offence if they could successfully show that 'the necessity' of alleviating suffering had overridden their duty to preserve life. The Supreme Court in 1984 endorsed the legitimacy of such decisions as 'justifying euthanasia'.[2] According to Marvin Newman it was agreed that a doctor who responded to a request for euthanasia would face no legal or professional hazard if he or she agreed to such a request under a number of given conditions.

> The first condition must be that there is clear and convincing evidence of enduring free determination by the patient so that there is no doubt at all of the patient's wish for his or her life to be ended. Second the patient's decision must be an informed one, made after full discussion with the doctors and in awareness of all relevant facts. Third the patient must face irreversible, protracted and unbearable suffering. And finally there must be, from the patient's viewpoint, an absence of reasonable alternatives to alleviate the suffering.[3]

When euthanasia was practised in such conditions, no doctor in the Netherlands was successfully prosecuted.

Claims of a slippery slope in the Netherlands

Opponents of voluntary euthanasia claim that its permissibility in the Netherlands led to two kinds of 'slippage', especially in the period before it was finally legalized. The first kind of slippage involved extending the meaning of 'unbearable suffering' beyond cases of terminal illness; the second is the claim that the existence of voluntary euthanasia led to a climate in which some leading politicians and health care experts called for much more liberal laws and where involuntary euthanasia was actually also being practised. Are these claims true?

Nigel Biggar gives two instances where the meaning of unbearable suffering had been extended. He says that the Dutch Supreme Court in 1994 found that 'unbearable suffering' could legitimately cover the inconsolable and persistent grief of a mother mourning the loss of both her sons. He also cites the case of a court in Haarlem in 2000 that extended the defence of 'irreversible protracted and unbearable suffering' to an otherwise healthy man who had sought euthanasia simply because he felt his life 'empty and pointless'.[4]

Neither of these cases supports this contention. In the case of the inconsolable mother it is not the case that the Supreme Court acquitted Dr Chabot for agreeing to give Mrs Bosscher assistance to die. The Court actually found him guilty of unlawful killing, but decided not to send him to prison. Likewise, the medical disciplinary council censured him for unprofessional behaviour, though it did not prevent him from continuing to practise. Both the courts and the medical profession made it absolutely clear that Dr Chabot's conduct was not acceptable and could not be used as a precedent. But they noted that Mrs Bosscher had undergone a most unhappy marriage that had ended in divorce. Subsequent to this her life had revolved around her two sons. But following the suicide of her elder son, the death of her father, and the death from cancer of her younger son she felt her life had become utterly unbearable. She had lost every human being who mattered to her, and having failed to commit suicide on her own she repeatedly begged Dr Chabot to provide her with pills with which she could end her life. After consulting with her GP and two psychiatric colleagues, Dr Chabot reluctantly felt he should accede to her request.[5] In these tragic circumstances the Supreme Court imposed no punishment on Dr Chabot. Precisely the same course would almost certainly have been followed by the British courts. Dr Penney Lewis points out that in the UK 'of 22 mercy-killing cases between 1982 and 1991 only one defendant was convicted of murder'. In all other cases charges were downgraded to lesser offences, resulting in probation or suspended sentences.[6] Hence the fact that Dr Chabot escaped a custodial sentence in the Netherlands does not mean that Dutch law 'approved' his action any more than comparably light sentences in Britain imply legal approval of mercy-killings here.

The second case is even less relevant because, as Professor Biggar acknowledges, the judgement of the Haarlem Court in 2000 that had justified the euthanasia of a man who felt life 'empty and pointless' was reversed on appeal in 2002. The Supreme Court ruled that 'unbearable suffering without prospect of improvement must be linked to a medical or psychiatric condition'.[7] This view was further endorsed and strengthened in the 2001 Termination of Life on Request Act that finally gave parliamentary approval for euthanasia but only on the strictest interpretation of earlier rulings, showing that a carefully drafted euthanasia law can provide greater safeguards than when law is shaped by individual court cases.

Non-voluntary euthanasia in the Netherlands

Opponents of legalizing assisted dying often argue that in the Netherlands the permissibility of euthanasia has led to a situation where many patients are killed or allowed to die without any reference to the tight conditions under which alone euthanasia is supposed to be permitted. Baroness Finlay claims that sometimes 'requests for euthanasia are generated by the family, or instigated by the physician without the expressed wish of the patient'.[8] Nigel Biggar highlights the fact that the Royal Dutch Medical Association has 'condoned the termination in certain circumstances of incompetent patients including babies and patients in persistent coma'.[9] John Keown notes that many people eminent in Dutch medical life have suggested that very old people living alone who are simply 'tired of life' should be allowed to obtain a suicide pill, and that a debate is starting in the Netherlands about whether euthanasia or assisted suicide should be generally available for those who have the beginnings of dementia. Keown believes that such discussions could be paving the way for a move to non-voluntary euthanasia.[10] The existence of non-voluntary euthanasia in the Netherlands has already been confirmed by three national surveys exploring the extent of medical behaviour that leads to the 'ending of life without explicit request'. In 1990 a survey showed that 0.8 per cent of deaths fell into this category, though in 1995 and 2001 this number had decreased to 0.7 per cent of all deaths.[11] The 1990 figure of around 1000 deaths brought about by non-voluntary euthanasia is repeatedly cited by opponents of voluntary euthanasia as evidence that a slippery slide from voluntary to non-voluntary euthanasia has occurred in the Netherlands and therefore could be expected to happen in Britain.

Is non-voluntary euthanasia in the Netherlands caused by 'slippage'?

Dr Penney Lewis shows that the slippery slope argument is flawed because it omits two vital considerations. First, the argument could only work if it could be shown that it was the permissive attitude to euthanasia that had *caused* the slippage; and second, this argument could only be effective if the slope had been 'more slippery' in the Netherlands than in jurisdictions where euthanasia was not permitted.

In her earlier analysis of the situation in the Netherlands, Margaret Otlowski pointed out that, according to the Royal Dutch Medical Association and the Dutch Society for Health Law, opponents of euthanasia have conveyed 'a very inaccurate and unreliable impression about the extent and nature of the practice of voluntary euthanasia in that country' and that 'voluntary euthanasia is in fact performed much less frequently than had earlier been thought'.[12] If we think back to the cases cited by Nigel Biggar or the views expressed by eminent Dutch leaders cited by Keown, the most important fact is that the Supreme Court struck down the idea that being 'tired of life' could be a ground for euthanasia, and that the Termination of Life on Request Act makes it very clear that to terminate a life without such a request is not euthanasia but murder.[13]

That some outspoken people in the Netherlands would like a much wider freedom to practise euthanasia is irrelevant. The same would be true of some eminent people in all comparable countries whether or not their laws allow euthanasia. Equally the fact that that there are cases in the Netherlands where desperately ill newborn babies are allowed to die, and cases where people who have been in a coma for a long time sometimes have their support systems switched off, does not indicate any slide down a slippery slope. Such issues arise in all advanced countries. Desperately ill neonates (babies less than one month old) and persons in a persistent vegetative state are legally allowed to die in Britain despite the fact that euthanasia is banned here. This is because it is rightly believed that such issues raise very different moral issues than the issue of 'voluntary euthanasia on request'.

What about the 1000 non-voluntary deaths reported in the Netherlands each year?

John Keown ignores the distinction between euthanasia and the issue of switching off life-support machines for newborn babies and people in a coma when he discusses the Dutch surveys. He argues that the three Dutch surveys provide us with the 'chilling statistic' that every year in the Netherlands lethal injections 'are administered to around 1000 patients without, as the law requires, an explicit request by the patient'. Keown acknowledges that of the 1000 deaths reported by the Remmelink Commission in 1990, 50 per cent of those killed were incompetent (as for instance in a coma), 15 per cent were newborn babies, 10 per cent were unable to give consent for other reasons and there were also 25 per cent who 'could have made a request for euthanasia, but did not do so'.[14]

Keown's language is extreme. No one would give a lethal injection to a person in a coma rather than simply switching off the life-support machine, and equally 99 per cent of desperately handicapped neonates are simply allowed to die rather than being kept alive artificially.[15] Hence the only category that could seriously be thought of as 'slippage' from voluntary euthanasia could be the 250 people apparently given assistance to die without an explicit request. However, we have to be careful here. Penney Lewis has shown that detailed Dutch investigations of these particular cases show that in all competent cases there was evidence of earlier discussion of euthanasia with the patient or an earlier expressed wish for euthanasia. Sixty-five per cent died from being given morphine for relief of their pain, and only 8 per cent from the muscle relaxant normally used for euthanasia. Almost all cases involved patients with only a few hours or days to live.[16] Moreover, before we can attribute *any* of these cases to slippage from the requirements of the Netherlands' provisions safe-guarding voluntary euthanasia we have to ask how such figures compare with statistics for similar end-of-life decisions made in countries where voluntary euthanasia is forbidden.

Why doctors have to make end-of-life decisions

The complexities of modern medicine mean that, apart from the small minority of people who die suddenly, death today is nor-mally a fairly prolonged matter. Because of this, whatever the law of a particular country may say about euthanasia, doctors have the unenviable task of making end-of-life decisions on behalf of, or in consultation with, their patients. We have already noted that according to Dr Mervyn Singer, Director of the Bloomsbury Institute of Intensive Care Medicine, most deaths in intensive care units in Britain happen, not because the body packs up, but because the doctors present decide there is no longer any point in trying to resist the inevitable, and switch off the life-support systems.[17] It is also the case that caring doctors are unwilling to allow patients to suffer needlessly in their final hours and are there-fore willing to provide alleviation of pain and of other symptoms, 'foreseeing but not intending' that this will have the side effect of shortening the patient's life. Because of these factors it is simply the case that 'medical decisions concerning the end of life . . . are . . . a part of modern medicine, and we had better openly dis-cuss them'.[18]

The findings of Clive Seale relating to end-of-life decisions in various countries

Professor Clive Seale has compared end-of-life decisions in seven European countries and has also looked at comparable data from Australia and New Zealand. These comparative surveys slightly inflate the percentage of end-of-life decisions by excluding 'sudden and unexpected deaths' where in the nature of the case doctors were not in a position to make, or not to make, any decision. Looking at these non-sudden deaths in seven European countries it is clear that the large majority of them follow decisions made by doctors. Switzerland has the highest proportion of such deaths at 75 per cent followed by the UK with 70.2 per cent. Both are significantly higher than the situation in the Netherlands (65.4 per cent) and Belgium (59 per cent) where voluntary euthanasia is actually permitted. End-of life decisions are also made in Denmark (61.1 per cent) and Sweden (50.9 per cent). Only in Italy (32.5 per cent) will the majority of people die without their end-of-life decision being made by an attending doctor.[19]

In the UK (and indeed in the other countries covered) the most significant decision is that of alleviating a patient's symptoms with possible life-shortening effect. This happened in 36.3 per cent of non-sudden UK deaths. In another 33.4 per cent of cases, death followed a decision to withhold or withdraw treatment. Doctor-assisted dying comprised 0.54 per cent of cases, 0.17 per cent were voluntary euthanasia and 0.36 per cent followed from a decision to end life without an explicit request from a patient. Taking the last three categories together we can conclude that only 1.07 per cent of non-sudden UK deaths would be described by the doctors concerned as owing to a form of euthanasia. If one includes sudden and unexpected deaths in these statistics in order to cover the whole population, then the proportion of deaths owing to a form of euthanasia drops to 0.49 per cent of all deaths and of these, owing to euthanasia, 0.16 per cent were voluntary and 0.33 per cent were non-voluntary. Similarly, the proportion of deaths owing to alleviation of symptoms drops to 32.8 per cent and from non-treatment decisions to 30.3 per cent.

Taking both sets of statistics together we can say that in the UK 63.1 per cent of all deaths and 67.7 per cent of non-sudden deaths were the result of end-of-life decisions arising from alleviating symptoms or non-treatment, and only 0.49 per cent of all deaths and 1.07 per cent of non-sudden deaths were owing to some form of euthanasia. A large majority of doctors attach great importance to making a clear distinction between the tiny proportion they would describe as arising from a form of euthanasia and the large majority of deaths that flow from either withholding treatment or from alleviating symptoms.

If we look at the questions actually asked, however, the distinction does not appear to be of much actual significance. The questions asked about end-of-life decisions were:

> Did you or a colleague withhold or withdraw treatment taking into account the probability or certainty that this action would hasten the end of a patient's life or with the explicit intention of not pro-longing death or hastening the end of life?

> Did you or a colleague intensify the alleviation of pain and/or symptoms using morphine or a comparable drug taking into account the probability or certainty that this action would hasten the end of a patient's life or partly with the intention of hastening the patient's life?

Reflecting on such questions makes one realize that the extent to which 'euthanasia' happens in any country with an advanced medical service is partly at least a question of preferred semantics. As John Griffiths points out,

> to a considerable extent a doctor can choose how to bring about a shortening of his patient's life and how to describe what it is that he has done. If one of the possibilities is unattractive . . . because it is illegal, he can accomplish the same result in a different way or under a different name.[20]

In other words, where euthanasia is forbidden, the doctor will des-cribe the death as owing to abstention from treatment or through giving pain relief. End-of-life decisions still have to be made, and in the majority of cases involving terminally ill patients they are made in the same kinds of way. Thus in the Netherlands, despite the fact that voluntary euthanasia is legal, 60.2 per cent of end-of-life decisions involve either non-treatment or allevia-tion of symptoms. Equally in Switzerland, though assisted dying is legal, the vast majority of doctors choose the route of non-treatment or of alleviating pain via morphine, knowing it may shorten life.

Helga Kuhse believes that:

Laws prohibiting the intentional termination of life, but permitting the withholding or withdrawing of treatment and the administration of life-shortening palliative care, do not prevent doctors from intentionally ending the lives of some of their patients. There are also good reasons to believe that such laws . . . encourage . . . unconsented to termination of patient's lives.[21]

The impact of euthanasia laws on consultation with patients

The most significant difference between 'permissive' countries where euthanasia or assisted dying are allowed and 'non-permissive' countries where they are not is in the level of involvement of the patient and of the patient's relatives in the end-of-life decision. In permissive European countries (Switzerland, Belgium and the Netherlands), competent patients will be drawn into the discussion in 81 per cent of cases and their relatives in 76.6 per cent of cases. In non-permissive European countries (Italy, Denmark and Sweden), the patients will be consulted in 49.5 per cent of cases and their relatives in 45.6 per cent of cases. Britain occupies a midway position: the patient will be consulted in 69 per cent of cases and the patient's relatives in 43.7 per cent.[22] Professor Seale thinks this is because, though euthanasia is forbidden in Britain, palliative care is highly developed here and hence there is greater consultation in Britain, though not as much as in countries where both palliative care and euthanasia are permitted. Seale's research understates the difference between permissive and non-permissive countries by grouping the three permissive countries and the three non-permissive countries together and including Belgium in the 'permissive'. The research he cites was actually carried out before euthanasia was legalized in Belgium and this pulls down the overall 'permissive figures' substantially; Belgium at 67 per cent was lower than the UK at 69 per cent and very much lower than in the two countries that were 'permissive' at the time of the survey (Switzerland at 78 per cent and the Netherlands at 92 per cent).[23] What I thought was the most significant finding in the original research was this figure of 92 per cent of doctors in the Netherlands who discuss end-of-life decisions with their patients.

In the 'non-permissive' countries there is also a major difficulty about just how open any discussion can be when euthanasia is actually illegal. The doctor may be willing to give a very high dose of morphine, 'foreseeing but not intending' that in addition to killing the pain it will also kill the patient. But the doctor cannot directly offer the patient that particular choice in a country where euthanasia is forbidden. The doctor has to be even more circumspect with the relatives. No doubt a sensitive physician can pick up vibes about what is really wanted, but inevitably misunderstandings can easily arise. Helga Kuhse comments that where 'existing laws prohibit the intentional termination of life, doctors are reluctant to discuss medical end-of-life decisions with their patients lest these decisions be construed as collaboration in euthanasia'.[24]

Euthanasia and trust between doctor and patient

Opponents of euthanasia in Britain frequently suggest that if euthanasia became permissible here it would undermine trust between doctors and patients. It is hard to see why this should be thought to be the case. At present a British doctor has to intuit what the patient really wants in relation to an end-of-life decision and has to make the ultimate decision on the patient's behalf. Real trust between doctor and patient only becomes fully possible when the full range of choices includes euthanasia, and therefore open discussion can take place about the true wishes of the patient. That is why 79 per cent of Britons say that they would trust their doctors more or the same if euthanasia were actually legalized.[25] They are sensible to think this, because if we look at countries where euthanasia or assisted dying are legal, such as Switzerland, Belgium or the Netherlands, we find that doctors are more, not less, trusted by their patients than in countries where euthanasia is forbidden. According to a report cited by Professor Raymond Tallis, former Chair of the Ethics committee of the Royal College of Physicians, the country where doctors are trusted most out of the seven countries surveyed is the Netherlands where euthanasia has been legal for longest.[26] In fact the figure for confidence in GPs in the Netherlands was a staggering 97 per cent primarily because the Dutch patients felt that their GPs took them seriously and provided them with proper information.

Helga Kuhse and Peter Singer think that the primary benefit of the legalization of euthanasia in the Netherlands is that it has enabled doctor and patient to talk freely through all the options available. This has had the valuable consequence that 'the open practice of voluntary euthanasia may have reduced the incidence of doctors acting without the consent of the patient in ways that the doctor foresees will result in the patient's death'.[27] This judgement was echoed by an editorial in the *British Medical Journal* for 29 September 2007 that found that patients are more likely to be killed by doctors without their consent in European countries where euthanasia is illegal than in countries like the Netherlands where euthanasia is legal.

Evidence that voluntary euthanasia in the Netherlands has not led to non-voluntary euthanasia

Mary Warnock and Elisabeth Macdonald argue that there is no evidence to show that legalizing voluntary euthanasia in the Netherlands has encouraged non-voluntary euthanasia. On the contrary, they think it 'plausible to argue that the existence of a law on the statute book spelling out the conditions under which alone assisted dying was permissible would itself act as a block to prevent descent down the slope and would make it less likely rather than more likely that non-voluntary euthanasia would take place'.[28] Nigel Biggar accepts that the consequence of the passing of the Termination of Life on Request Act of 2001 involved 'a significant measure of movement *up* the Dutch slope'.[29]

In her encyclopaedic survey, *Voluntary Euthanasia and the Common Law*, in 1997, Margaret Otlowski exhaustively examined all the evidence available at that time concerning the social impact of legalizing voluntary euthanasia. Her conclusion relating to the Netherlands was unequivocal: 'There is no indication that active euthanasia on request is practised more often in the Netherlands than elsewhere.'[30]

A similar conclusion has been arrived at ten years later by Dr Penney Lewis in what is the most detailed, exhaustive and fully referenced discussion of all the available evidence today. She too argues that there is no evidence that non-voluntary euthanasia has increased because of the legalization of the voluntary in the either the Netherlands or Belgium or Oregon. The supposition that it would have this consequence is simply not supported by the available empirical evidence.[31] In addition to the evidence from her which I have previously discussed I note the important fact that the rate of non-voluntary euthanasia in some Western jurisdictions that have not (or had not) legalized euthanasia is significantly higher than in the Netherlands. Thus in 1996 Helga Kuhse found that the rate of termination of life without explicit consent was 3.5 per cent of all Australian deaths.[32] A 1998 a survey for the *Journal of the American Medical Association* found that of 335 oncologists interviewed in-depth 38 (slightly more than 10 per cent) had carried out either euthanasia or physician-assisted suicide (and this was before the State of Oregon made it legal in that one state).[33] In 1998, four years before euthanasia was legalized in Belgium, it was discovered that in Flanders 3.2 per cent of lives were ended without any explicit request.[34] These figures are between four and five times the level of such deaths in the Netherlands and tell strongly against the suggestion that non-voluntary deaths in the Netherlands were caused by its acceptance of voluntary euthanasia.

The impact of legalizing assisted suicide on vulnerable groups

One major concern about the impact of legalizing assisted dying is the effect it might have on vulnerable groups in our society who might experience a pressure to seek euthanasia for themselves. For example, the American College of Physicians is worried that 'the sick, the elderly, the poor, ethnic minorities and other vulnerable groups . . . might come to be further discounted by society, or even to view themselves as unproductive and burdensome and on that basis "appropriate" candidates for assistance with suicide'. The College also believed that 'patients with dementia, disabled persons . . . and those confronting costly chronic illness' would be placed at risk. This concern was shared by the British Medical Association, which likewise believed that legalizing euthanasia would 'put vulnerable people in the position of feeling they had to consider precipitating the end of their lives'.[35]

But we do not need to speculate about what the results of allow-ing euthanasia or assisted dying might be. In the Netherlands the Dutch Government has commissioned four nationwide studies covering all end-of-life decisions in the years 1990, 1995, 2001, 2005. There have also been a number of smaller focused Dutch studies which provide additional data. In Oregon the Department of Human Services has issued detailed annual reports ever since the Death with Dignity Act took place. There have also been three fur-ther surveys by Oregon physicians and hospice professionals. All this data has been meticulously analysed by a team of five scholars for the *Journal of Medical Ethics* and their detailed con-clusion is that, apart from people suffering from AIDS, people in 'vulnerable' groups were less likely than the population at large to make use of the assisted dying legislation. Aids sufferers might be considered as a special sub-group here in that characteristically they are likely to cherish their individual autonomy and right to decide for themselves on ethical issues. They are not dispropor-tionately drawn from the downtrodden, unemployed or poorly educated. Hence their profile is more like that of others who opt for assisted dying rather than from groups more self-evidently 'vulnerable' such as the old, the long-term disabled and the poor.

There is direct evidence that the very old are not inclined to seek out assistance to die. In Oregon persons aged 18 to 64 were over three times more likely to seek assisted suicide than people in the over-85 age group. (This finding by Margaret Battin's group has been further enhanced by the eighth report of the Department of Human Services in Oregon issued in March 2008, which found that the median age of those who died under the Death with Dignity Act in 2007 was only 65 years compared with a median age of 70 in previous years.) Margaret Battin and her team found that in the Netherlands also rates for voluntary euthanasia were lowest among the over-80s. Similarly, women, people with non-terminal physical disabilities or chronic illnesses, the uninsured, the poor, people with low educational attainment, and those from racial or ethnic minorities were all unlikely to seek euthanasia or assisted dying. In both Oregon and the Netherlands it is manifest that 'people who died with a physician's assistance were more likely to be members of groups enjoying comparative social, economic, educational, professional and other privileges'.[36]

What this data makes clear is that there is no empirical support to justify fears that legalizing assisted dying puts the vulnerable under pressure to seek it. It is not the vulnerable, but those who enjoy positions of responsibility, independence and personal autonomy who are likely to request help so that they can also exercise their autonomy in relation to the manner and timing of their deaths. Where external pressures have been felt by the patient, for example, from their families, these pressures have been 'in opposition to the patient's choice of assisted dying'. Indeed, according to Raymond Tallis, a professor of geriatrics, 'In Oregon, 25 per cent of terminally ill patients who were planning to have an assisted death, modified or delayed their plans at the family's request, even when this prolonged their sufferings.'[37]

The benefits of the Death with Dignity Act in Oregon

The supreme example of the success of a carefully drafted assisted dying bill is the Death with Dignity Act in Oregon on which Lord Joffe's UK Bill was modelled. The experience of Oregon shows that when adequate safeguards are in place there is no question at all of sliding down any slippery slopes. There is also no evidence to support another fear often expressed by opponents of assisted dying, namely, that if assisted dying were readily available this would put in jeopardy pressure to provide good palliative care. Quite the reverse. The best evidence for this comes from the evidence submitted to the committee of inquiry into Lord Joffe's Bill by Ann Jackson, Executive Director and Chief Executive Officer of the Oregon Hospice Association.[38] This association like other hospice movements was worried that allowing assisted dying would threaten the expansion of good hospice development and lead to an avalanche of cases of people being put to death against their will. So the moment the Act was passed the Oregon Hospice Movement went to court to get it declared unconstitutional. They fought the Act all the way to the Federal Supreme Court of the USA. However, American legal processes are very slow, and it took eight years before the Supreme Court ruled. It ultimately came down in favour of the Act. 'Yes', it was constitutionally possible for a US State to allow assisted dying.

The intriguing thing is that at that point the Oregon Hospice Association drafted a new position statement that said that they were most relieved to have lost their case because to their surprise the hospice movement had benefited greatly from the Act and 'absolutely none of the dire consequences that had been predicted had occurred'.[39]

This judgement is echoed by the evidence to the House of Lords from Professor Raymond Tallis, who chaired the Committee on Ethical Issues in Medicine of the Royal College of Physicians until 2004. He reported that when his committee first discussed the Joffe Bill he had supported their decision to oppose it on the following series of assumptions:

> That good palliative care would obviate the need for assisted dying; that assisted dying legislation would stunt the development of our current underdeveloped palliative care services; that there would be a slippery slope in which assisted dying would be extended to people who did not want it, or could not give informed consent particularly those vulnerable people who have been my main professional concern; and that it would break down trust between doctors and patients.

However, having carefully examined the empirical evidence from the Netherlands and Oregon Professor Tallis changed his mind entirely and became a strong supporter of the Joffe Bill because:

Every single one of those assumptions has proved to be false in those countries where assisted dying is available. Indeed the impact of liberalising legislation has proved to be the reverse of what I had assumed.[40]

What people really want from assisted dying legislation

What really changed in Oregon because of the Death with Dignity Act was that over those eight years there had been a massive increase in the number of people who died in hospices (from 22 per cent to 51 per cent), plus the highest proportion of people who obtain their wish to die in their own homes of any state in America.[41] Ann Jackson claimed that this is why *Forbes* magazine identified Oregon as one of the best places to die in all the USA. It is interesting that despite the ready availability of assisted dying only 0.14 per cent of Oregonians have ultimately chosen an assisted death. In practice few people really want assistance to die. This does not mean that legalizing assisted dying is unnecessary because what people definitely do want is the peace of mind that comes from knowing that assistance to die will be available to them if their suffering really does remain unbearable.

According to Ann Jackson: 'Only 1 of 200 individuals who consider a request, and 1 in 25 of these who formally make a request, will actually use a prescription.'[42] Even those who go through the full procedure and obtain the necessary prescription for the wherewithal to end their lives do not always go through with it. Of 85 prescriptions for lethal medications written out in 2007 only 46 took the medication, 26 died naturally from their underlying disease and 13 were still alive by the end of the year.[43] What these figures show is that what most people want from assisted dying legislation is not death, but reassurance that assistance to die will be given if their situation continues to develop in a way that is utterly unbearable to them. Ann Jackson believes that in Oregon the Death with Dignity Act provides great comfort for these patients without them actually having to use the Act. 'Hospices have reported that once patients have a plan for their worst-case scenario, they are better able to get on with their lives.'[44]

This is also the case in the Netherlands, where 'a large number of patients seek assurance from their doctors that active voluntary euthanasia will be available if the suffering becomes intolerable',[45] but relatively few go on to take advantage of this. According to Ruurd Veldhuis, in 1995, 34,500 people took the precaution of going through the necessary legal procedures to enable them to receive euthanasia 'when time would come'. But of these, only 3,200, less than 10 per cent of those who had obtained approval, ultimately did go ahead with it.[46]

Why Christians should welcome these developments

I believe that to give people the peace of mind that comes from knowing that they will be able to release themselves from their suffering if it proves really unbearable is a wonderful reassurance to offer to the dying. It helps them to make the best of what remains of their life. Just to know that the right exists brings them a sense of assurance and a peace of mind that enables them to cope better with their illness. They change from being simply victims of circumstance to persons who know they have some control over their destiny if their worst fears about the course of their illness come to be realized. What the people of Oregon and the Netherlands value is living in a society where they are free to be, as far as possible, responsible for their own lives, and free to make their own decisions as to what treatment or help they wish to have. This includes the right to choose between adequate hospice care in the terminal stages of illness, or the equal right to seek for medical assistance to help them move on to what Christians believe will be the fuller life of the world to come. I believe that any who believe that they ought to seek to show forth the love of God in their lives ought to be the first, not the last, to welcome such provisions.

10

A Christian case for assisted dying

The need to build on Christian foundations

If one is attempting to make a Christian case for any position it is axiomatic that one must attempt to build on a foundation of Christian belief, and in allegiance to the teaching and example of Jesus Christ. This is a hazardous task because history is full of examples of people who have claimed the authority of Christ and his religion for deeds and practices that might with more truth be assigned to almost any other source.[1] The attempt has to be made, however, if we are seeking to answer the question: 'Is there a *Christian* case for assisted dying?' The attempt is all the more necessary because the authority of Christianity is normally claimed by opponents of euthanasia, even though they rarely appeal to Christian premises in public debate.

Why Christian opponents of euthanasia rarely appeal to Christian premises

Nigel Biggar, whose book *Aiming to Kill* presents the strongest case I know against euthanasia, is a Christian priest and Regius Professor of Moral Theology at the University of Oxford. Yet he rarely alludes directly to any Christian sources. He acknowledges that his book contains 'barely a single handful of direct references to the text of the Bible' and that some Christians might think that his approach 'can hardly be truly Christian'.[2] The powerful case he makes against euthanasia derives from his conviction that a slippery slope would be inevitable. The same is true of Professor Stephen Williams who wrote a chapter replying to me in *Facing Death*. My chapter was called 'Theology and the case for euthanasia'. His was called simply 'The case against euthanasia', and he says explicitly that though he writes 'as a Christian by conviction and a theologian by profession . . . moral reasoning involves attending to the conceptual dimensions of issues in a way that is not specifically theological or religious'. Williams acknowledges that if one really did start from Christian premises, such as Jesus' Golden Rule one could not 'rule out euthanasia' because mercy killing in particular cases can indeed be justified by Jesus' own teaching. However, Williams goes on to assert that this fact provides no warrant for making voluntary euthanasia part of medical practice, for if one once did that he believes it would be 'difficult to ward off non-voluntary euthanasia'.[3]

Basing euthanasia on Jesus' Golden Rule

In the footnotes to his article, Stephen Williams notes that the distinguished moral philosopher, Professor R. M. Hare, said of the prescriptions of Jesus' Golden Rule: 'I can think of no moral question on which they have a more direct bearing than the question of euthanasia.'[4] Hare's argument seems logically impeccable. Jesus taught that the heart of all morality is to treat other people as we wish to be treated ourselves. According to a YouGov survey of 10 March 2008, 76 per cent of respondents agreed, or agreed strongly, that terminally ill people should be allowed medical assistance to die.[5] We noted in Chapter 4 that doctors are more likely than others to seek this way out. Doctors plan euthanasia for themselves and three-quarters of the population agree that the terminally ill should be given assistance to die; so if we apply the Golden Rule it is clear that doctors should be permitted to treat their patients as they intend to treat themselves and as the majority of the population wishes to be treated.

Jesus' summary of what is essential to religious law

When Jesus was asked what was the greatest commandment of all his response was:

> You shall love the Lord your God with all your heart, and with all your soul, and with all your mind. This is the first and great commandment. And a second is like it, You shall love your neighbour

as yourself. On these two commandments depend all the law and prophets. (Matt. 22.37–40)

Many Christians claim that the Bible is their guide to moral judgement. If so, it is to these verses that they should look most closely for guidance. After all, Christians are essentially meant to be followers of Jesus Christ. His teaching that these two commandments summarize all that is essential in religious law and prophetic teaching is something that Christians should take with the utmost seriousness.

Euthanasia and loving God with heart, soul and mind

For a person who loves God with heart, soul and mind, death is not the ultimate disaster. Death is the gateway to eternal life with God. At death we commit ourselves into the loving hands of God. We can do this in confidence, for Jesus taught that God, like a loving father, will always rejoice in giving a welcome to his prodigal children.[6] According to Cardinal Basil Hume's picture of life as a pilgrimage towards God, words like 'hope', 'expectation' and 'looking forward to the vision of God' should characterize a Christian's thoughts of death and dying. 'This should be a cause of peace, a cause of joy; one day forward, one step nearer.'[7] In his reflections on the death of Diana, Princess of Wales, the cardinal spoke of her as now 'locked for ever in God's ecstatic love'.[8] When Cardinal Hume was diagnosed with terminal cancer he rang to tell Timothy Wright, the then Abbot of Ampleforth. The abbot said: 'Congratulations! That's brilliant news. I wish I was coming with you.'[9]

Such a sentiment is highly unusual today, though it would have been commonplace in the first three centuries of the Christian era. Yet, as the example of the Abbot of Ampleforth reminds us, there are still many Christians for whom the Christian hope is a living reality. It was a reality to the great twentieth-century theologian Dietrich Bonhoeffer. As he was being taken away to be hanged, he said, 'This is the end. For me the beginning of life.'[10] He sincerely believed that 'Death is the supreme festival on the road to freedom.'[11] It is important that Bonhoeffer thought this, because more than almost any other twentieth-century theologian he also taught by both word and deed how important it was for Christians to immerse themselves fully in the life of this world and to thankfully enjoy all the blessings that life gives us. However, his stress on the value and goodness of human life and the importance of 'this-worldliness' was always rooted in his conviction that it was also *essential* that we should never forget that ultimately 'this poor earth is not our home' and hence he never regretted the imminence of his own martyrdom.[12]

It is utterly paradoxical that today it is Christians who are characteristically seen as clinging to life, whereas in the early Church St Athanasius believed that the most convincing argument for belief in the resurrection of Jesus was the fact that Christians 'treat death as nothing . . . they go eagerly to meet it . . . rather than remain in this present life'.[13] This is the genuinely Christian approach to the understanding of life. It would be good if it could once more be the case, as it was for the earliest Christians, that an assisted suicide at the very end of a fulfilled life could once again be described as 'a noble death'. It would also be an act of faith and trust, giving back to God the life we owe to him.

Euthanasia and loving one's neighbour as oneself

The importance of outgoing unselfish, loving compassion for others is often claimed as one of the greatest contributions that Christianity has given to the world. This particular kind of love, identified through the Greek word *agape*, differs from both *eros* (romantic or sexual love) and *philia* (the love of friends). It is celebrated in St Paul's great hymn to love in 1 Corinthians 13, one of the best loved of all biblical passages. It is highly relevant to the euthanasia debate. The sole context in which we are discussing voluntary euthanasia is when a person is suffering unbearably during their terminal illness and repeatedly begs for assistance to die. It is hard to see how anyone who takes St Paul's praise of loving compassion seriously could fail to respond to the desperate cries for help witnessed by Dr Julia Lawton in her account of individual patients' experiences of palliative care. Among the more tragic were Christine, suffering from unrelievable chronic diarrhoea, which made her describe life in the hospice as 'the nearest thing to hell on earth', or Kath who begged for permanent sedation because 'no one would put a dog through this' or Roz who experienced the hospice as a 'death factory'.[14]

When people's sufferings are so great that they make repeated requests to die, it seems a denial of that loving compassion, which is supposed to be the hallmark of Christianity, to refuse to allow their requests to be granted. If we truly love our neighbour as ourselves how can we deny them the death we would wish for ourselves in such a condition? We might also ask the Revd Baroness (Kathleen) Richardson of Calow's searching question to opponents of euthanasia: 'By what moral judgement can we justify keeping alive those people who sincerely want to die, when their life is in their own eyes not worth preserving?'[15] We might also note that St Paul believed that 'love does not insist on its own way'. This suggests that love might require us to assist a person to die if that were their wish even if it were not ours.

Is terminal sedation significantly different from euthanasia?

Baroness Warnock and Elisabeth Macdonald point out that in 48 per cent of cases people will receive 'terminal sedation' so that they are unconscious long before death and do not have to suffer any longer.[16] But in whose interest is this alternative seen as preferable? Dr Julia Lawton suggests that sedation is 'performed primarily to reinforce the hospice's ideology of a good death ... which requires the presence of "docile bodies" within communal space'. However, 'in removing a patient's sentience through sedation the last vestiges of their personhood are also erased'.[17] From the point of view of the dying patient life effectively ends when permanent sedation begins rather than when he or she finally breathes out for the last time perhaps several weeks later.

Euthanasia and Christian empiricism

In Chapter 5 we noted that Christians who oppose any change in the euthanasia law normally do so because they are frightened of the consequences that they fear might follow. I argued in the previous chapter that the actual consequences of euthanasia legislation in the Netherlands and in Oregon have turned out to be wholly beneficial, particularly in the greatly increased trust and confidence placed in the medical profession. I drew attention to how bitterly the Oregon Hospice Association had fought against the Death with Dignity Act, but also how after seeing it in practice for eight years they recognized that none of their fears had been realized and that the situation of the terminally ill had been dramatically improved. A comparable change of mood took place in the Netherlands. When euthanasia was first mooted there in 1966 it was deeply controversial and was opposed by 49 per cent of the population. After 30 years' experience of how the law worked only 10 per cent continued to oppose it in 1996.[18] Today there is no talk of going back to the bad old days and the Netherlands' neighbours in Belgium and Luxembourg have subsequently sought to follow their lead.

I believe that on the basis of the evidence discussed in the previous chapter there is no empirical foundation for a Christian to fear the consequence of setting in place a well-worked-out euthanasia law like the Death with Dignity Act in Oregon. The same is also true if we consider the situation in Belgium. There, the first requirement of their euthanasia law is that the patient must be 'in a futile medical condition of constant physical or mental suffering that cannot be alleviated'.[19] When a person is in such a condition it is hard to see by what right any of us should deny a fellow human being the relief they seek. This is particularly the case if one seriously believes in the reality of eternal life with God as our ultimate destiny.

The death of Socrates

In the days when education was dominated by the Classics, many people found themselves attracted by Plato's description of the last days of Socrates.[20] Socrates had been condemned to death for attacking superstitious religious beliefs and was given the choice between death and exile from Athens. At his advanced age he chose death and his disciples and friends gathered round him for a last meeting. Socrates drank the hemlock and engaged in lively philosophical discussion with his friends until he gradually passed into unconsciousness. Many feel that this was a better way of dying than what we can expect today.

The desirability of a Christian deathbed

Historically it used to be the practice of all believers to summon a priest when death was thought near, so that the patient could be given the last rites, and die surrounded by an atmosphere of prayer and worship, as well as in the presence of family and friends. Modern technology has largely taken away that option. Most of us will die alone and often unconscious in a hospital bed so attached to saline drips and other support systems that the older deathbed scene ceases to be possible. Assisted dying legislation could restore the possibilities for a Christian deathbed. One could imagine a situation where a Christian could say goodbye to family and friends, a Holy Communion service could be celebrated at the believer's bedside, and he or she could be given the last rites in preparation for the journey through death to the life immortal. In a context of faith this would seem a more Christian way of death than the present lonely extension of the dying process.

A Christian prayer for a peaceful end

One of the oldest Christian prayers, generally attributed to St Ambrose, asks God for a peaceful end. In the hymn's translation it says:[21]

> Grant to life's day a calm unclouded ending,
>   An eve untouched by shadows of decay,
> The brightness of a holy death-bed blending
>   With dawning glories of the eternal day.

If this is the kind of death a Christian can legitimately ask for from God, should it not also be the kind of death the same person could request from a doctor as an agent of God's love in helping forward the realization of this prayer?

Notes

Introduction

1 BMA, Guidance <http://www.bmjpg.com/withwith/chapters/3a_l.htm>.
2 *Joint Submission from the Church of England House of Bishops and the Roman Catholic Bishops' Conference of England and Wales to the House of Lords Select Committee*, paragraph 17 <www.cofe.anglican.org/new/newsitem_item2004-10-19-9713099720>.
3 Mary Warnock and Elisabeth Macdonald, *Easeful Death: Is There a Case for Assisted Dying?* (Oxford: Oxford University Press, 2008), p. 137.
4 Julia Lawton, *The Dying Process* (London: Routledge, 2000); Guy Brown, *The Living End: The Future of Death, Aging and Immortality* (Basingstoke: Palgrave Macmillan, 2007); Mary Warnock and Elisabeth Macdonald, *Easeful Death: Is There a Case for Assisted Dying?* (Oxford: Oxford University Press, 2008); Clive Seale, 'Characteristics of End-of-life Decisions: Survey of UK Medical Practitioners', *Palliative Medicine*, 2006, pp. 653–9, and 'National Survey of End-of-life Decisions Made by UK Medical Practitioners', *Palliative Medicine*, 2006, pp. 3–10; Penney Lewis, *Assisted Dying and Legal Change* (Oxford: Oxford University Press, 2007).

1 Why theology matters in the euthanasia debate

1 House of Lords, *Report of the Select Committee on Medical Ethics* (London: HMSO, 31 January 1994), p. 24.
2 House of Lords, *Report of the Select Committee on Medical Ethics*, p. 48.
3 Paul Badham, 'MCU Submission on the Assisted Dying Bill', *Modern Believing*, 46.1, April 2005, pp. 46–51.
4 *The Times*, 31 March 2008.
5 Hans Küng and Walter Jens, *A Dignified Dying: A Plea for Personal Responsibility* (London: SCM Press, 1995).
6 Joseph Fletcher, *Situation Ethics: The New Morality* (London: SCM Press), 1966.
7 Robin Gill (ed.), *Euthanasia and the Churches* (London: Cassell, 1998), p. 21.
8 Dignity in Dying, *The Report* (London: Dignity in Dying, 2006), p. 14.
9 Gill, *Euthanasia and the Churches*, p. 19.

2 Why euthanasia and assisted dying have become major issues of concern

1 Earlier figures from Patrick Nowell Smith, 'The Right to Die', in Paul Badham (ed.), *Ethics on the Frontiers of Human Existence* (New York: Paragon House, 1992), pp. 209–21, 215, later figures from Dignity in Dying, *The Report* (London: Dignity in Dying, 2006), p. 14, citing a range of NOP and YouGov polls.

2 Guy Brown, *The Living End: The Future of Death, Aging and Immortality* (Basingstoke: Palgrave Macmillan, 2007), pp. 27–30.

3 Hans Küng and Walter Jens, *A Dignified Dying: A Plea for Personal Responsibility* (London: SCM Press, 1995), pp. 32–3.

4 Brown, *Living End*, pp. 25 and 60.

5 Brown, *Living End*, pp. 74 and 218.

6 Richard Nicholson, 'Radical Surgery Needed – Cut Out the Hospitals', *The Times*, 6 October 2006.

7 Mary Warnock and Elisabeth Macdonald, *Easeful Death: Is There a Case for Assisted Dying?* (Oxford: Oxford University Press, 2008), p. 126.

8 Brown, *Living End*, pp. 74–5 and 39.

9 Consumers' Association, 'The Cost of Care', *Which?*, April 2008, pp. 34–7.

10 *Sunday Times*, 2 March 2008.

11 *The Times*, 26 April 2008.

12 Warnock and Macdonald, *Easeful Death*, p. 127.

13 Dan Cohn-Sherbok and Lavinia Cohn-Sherbok, *What Do You Do When Your Parents Live for Ever?* (Ropley: O Books, 2007).

14 Brown, *Living End*, p. 75, citing J. Addington-Hall, D. Altmann and M. McCarthy in *Age and Ageing*, 27, 1998, pp. 129–36. Cf. Julia Addington-Hall and Mark McCarthy, 'Dying from Cancer: Results of a National Population Based Investigation', *Palliative Medicine*, 9.4, 1995, pp. 295–305.

15 Brown, *Living End*, pp. 93 and 221.

16 David Oliver, ' "Acopia" and "Social Admission" Are Not Diagnoses: Why Older People Deserve Better', *Journal of the Royal Society of Medicine*, 101.4, April 2008, pp. 168–74 (Acopia means 'inability to cope').

17 W. Shakespeare, *Hamlet* III.i.69.

18 Nowell Smith, 'Right to Die', pp. 211–12.

19 Clive Seale in *The Times Higher Educational Supplement*, 6 January 1995, p. 16.

20 Hans Küng and Walter Jens, *A Dignified Dying: A Plea for Personal Responsibility* (London: SCM Press, 1995), p. 31.

21 Douglas James Davies, *A Brief History of Death* (Oxford: Blackwell, 2005), p. 205.

22 Elaine Murphy, 'Effectiveness of Palliative Care: A Position Paper', October 2006, cited in a briefing note sent to me, 21 May 2008, from Carmen Dupont, Policy and Information Officer of Dignity in Dying.

23 M. S. Rogers and C. J. Todd, 'The Right Kind of Pain: Talking about Symptoms in Outpatient Oncology Consultations', *Palliative Medicine*, 14, 2000, pp. 299–307.

24 Arthur Hugh Clough, 'The Latest Decalogue' (1862).

25 Alastair Campbell, 'Euthanasia and the Principle of Justice', in Robin Gill, *Euthanasia and the Churches* (London: Cassell, 1998), pp. 83–97, 83–7 and cf. p. 100.

26 Warnock and Macdonald, *Easeful Death*, p. 107.

27 Cited in Warnock and Macdonald, *Easeful Death*, p. 62.

28 Nowell Smith, 'Right to Die', p. 219.

3 The personal dimension

1 Hans Küng and Walter Jens, *A Dignified Dying: A Plea for Personal Responsibility* (London: SCM Press, 1995), p. 25.

2 Erik L. Krakauer, 'Attending to Dying', in H. M. Spiro, M. G. McCrea Curnen and Lee Palmer Wandel, *Facing Death* (New Haven and London: Yale University Press, 1996), pp. 22–32, 24.

3 Sherwin Nuland, *How We Die* (London: Chatto & Windus, 1994), p. 233.

4 Nuland, *How We Die*, p. 256.

4 Euthanasia as discussed from 'absolutist' perspectives on morality

1 Pope John Paul II, *Catechism of the Catholic Church* (London: Chapman, 1994), p. 491.

2 <http://en.wikipedia.org/wiki/Hippocratic_Oath#The_original_oath>.

3 Thomas Aquinas, *Summa Theologia* Q. 64 Art. 5, cited on <www.philosophy.ed.ac.uk/ug_study/ug_intro/suiquot.pdf>.

4 Immanuel Kant, *Lectures on Ethics*, cited on <www.philosophy.ed.ac.uk/ug_study/ug_intro/suiquot.pdf>.

5 S. Korner, *Kant* (Harmondsworth: Penguin, 1966 [1955]), p. 136.

6 1 Samuel 15.3.

7 Leviticus 20.6, 27.

8 Numbers 15.33–36.

9 Exodus 21.17.

10 Leviticus 19.13.

11 Leviticus 19.10.

12 Leviticus 20.17.

13 Leviticus 20.18.

14 Deuteronomy 21.18.

15 Leviticus 21.9.

16 B. Bende, 'Letters: The Hippocratic Oath', *British Medical Journal* 309, 1994, 952.

17 <www.wma.net/e/policy/c8.htm>.

18 W. Shakespeare, *Hamlet* I.ii.129; III.i.69, 62–3.

19 Augustine, *City of God* 1.19.

20 Judges 17.28–30.

21 1 Samuel 31.3–6; 2 Samuel 1.11–27.

22 1 Maccabees 6.44.

23 Oregon Department of Human Services, *Seventh Annual Report on Oregon's Death with Dignity Act* (Oregon: Office of Disease Prevention and Epidemiology, 2005), p. 24.

24 Matthew 27.5; 26.24.

25 Arthur J. Droge and James D. Tabor, *A Noble Death: Suicide and Martyrdom among Jews and Christians in the Ancient World* (San Francisco: Harper SanFrancisco, 1992).

26 John 10.10–16.

27 Acts 20.16–38.

28 Droge and Tabor, *Noble Death*, p. 131.

29 Droge and Tabor, *Noble Death*, pp. 167–80, 154, 30.

30 'Trajan's Reply to Pliny', in J. Stevenson (ed.), *A New Eusebius: Documents Illustrative of the History of the Church to A.D. 337* (London: SPCK, 1963), p. 16.

31 Droge and Tabor, *Noble Death*, p. 154.

32 G. E. M. de Ste Croix, 'Aspects of the "Great" Persecution', *Harvard Theological Review*, 47, 1954, pp. 75–113, 102, cited in Droge and Tabor, *Noble Death*, p. 154.

33 Paul Middleton, *Radical Martyrdom and Cosmic Conflict in Early Christianity* (London: T&T Clark, 2006), p. 30.

34 Droge and Tabor, *Noble Death*, p. 159 note 10.

35 Droge and Tabor, *Noble Death*, p. 178.

36 Ecclesiasticus 41.1.

37 Mark 2.27.

38 Acts 26.5.

39 Galatians 5.1.
40 Six national polls since 2000 are cited in Dignity in Dying's *Report*, dated February 2006.
41 *Sunday Times*, 20 July 1997.
42 Mary Warnock and Elisabeth Macdonald, *Easeful Death: Is There a Case for Assisted Dying?* (Oxford: Oxford University Press, 2008), p. 122.
43 K. L. Vaux, 'Debbie's Dying: Mercy Killing and the Good Death', letter in the *Journal of the American Medical Association*, 259.14, 1988, pp. 2140–1.
44 Guy Brown, *The Living End: The Future of Death, Aging and Immortality* (Basingstoke: Palgrave Macmillan, 2007), p. 9.
45 Sherwin Nuland, *How We Die* (London: Chatto & Windus, 1994), p. 143.
46 Brown, *Living End*, p. 84.
47 Jeremy Taylor, *The Rules and Exercises of Holy Dying* (Oxford, 1651).
48 Julia Lawton, *The Dying Process: Patients' Experience of Palliative Care* (London: Routledge, 2000), as quoted in Brown, *Living End*, p. 79.
49 Paul Barry Clarke, 'Euthanasia', in Paul Barry Clarke and Andrew Linzey (eds), *Dictionary of Ethics, Theology and Society* (London: Routledge, 1996), p. 336.

5 Euthanasia from a consequentialist perspective

1 Joseph Butler, *Fifteen Sermons* (1726; London: Bell, 1964), p. 6.
2 Butler, *Fifteen Sermons*, p. 7.
3 Butler, *Fifteen Sermons*, p. 30.
4 I have failed to find this as a direct quotation. Typing the quote on to Google throws up Butler, *Sermon 3*, but I suspect it is a popular epitome of his argument here rather than a verbatim one.
5 D. M. MacKinnon, *A Study in Ethical Theory* (London: Adam & Charles Black, 1957), p. 177.
6 Butler, *Fifteen Sermons*, p. 171.
7 Butler, *Fifteen Sermons*, p. 40.
8 Matthew 7.12, REB; *Analects* 15.23.
9 For documentation, see Christie Davies, 'Religion, Politics and "Permissive" Legislation', in Paul Badham (ed.), *Religion, State and Society in Modern Britain* (Lewiston, NY, and Lampeter: Mellen, 1989), pp. 319–40, and Davies, 'How People Argue about Abortion and Capital Punishment and Why', in Badham (ed.), *Ethics on the Frontiers of Human Existence* (New York: Paragon House, 1992), pp. 101–36.

10 Joseph Fletcher, *Situation Ethics: The New Morality* (London: SCM Press, 1966).

11 Jeremy Bentham, *Principles of Morals and Legislation* (1781; New York: Prometheus, 1988).

12 John Stuart Mill, *Utilitarianism* (1861; Harmondsworth: Penguin, 1987).

13 Board for Social Responsibility of the Church of England, *On Dying Well* (1975; London: Church House Publishing, 2nd edn, 2000), p. 23, as cited in Nigel Biggar, *Aiming to Kill: The Ethics of Suicide and Euthanasia* (London: Darton, Longman & Todd, 2004), p. 143.

14 House of Lords, *Report of the Select Committee on Medical Ethics* (London: HMSO, 31 January 1994), p. 48.

15 House of Lords, *Report of the Select Committee on Medical Ethics*, paras 236–7.

16 Davies, 'Religion, Politics and "Permissive" Legislation', p. 321.

17 Church of England Board for Social Responsibility, *Putting Asunder* (London: SPCK, 1966).

18 Board for Social Responsibility, *Abortion: An Ethical Discussion* (London: Church Information Office, 1965).

19 Andrew Marr, *A History of Modern Britain* (London: Macmillan, 2007), p. 256.

20 Editorial, in *Theology*, July/August 1997, p. 241.

21 Sam Rowlands, 'Contraception and Abortion', *Journal of the Royal Society of Medicine*, 100, October 2007, p. 467.

22 Margaret Otlowski, *Voluntary Euthanasia and the Common Law* (Oxford: Clarendon Press, 1997), p. 223.

23 Robin Gill (ed.), *Euthanasia and the Churches* (London: Cassell, 1998), p. 38.

24 <www.cofe.anglican.org/news/news_item.2004-10-19.9713099720>.

25 *The Times*, 31 March 2008.

26 <www.parliamentaryprolife.org.uk/newsarchive/nick_individual-page.asp?NewsID=527>

27 Cited by Margaret Battin, Agnes van der Heide, Linda Ganzini, Gerrit van der Wal and Brejie Onwukteaka-Philkipsen, 'Legal Physician-assisted Dying in Oregon and The Netherlands: Evidence concerning the Impact on Patients in "Vulnerable" Groups', *Journal of Medical Ethics*, 33, 2007, pp. 591–7, 592.

28 Hans Küng and Walter Jens, *A Dignified Dying: A Plea for Personal Responsibility* (London: SCM Press, 1995), p. 20.

29 Biggar, *Aiming to Kill*, p. 159.

30 See, for example, Nicholas Goodrick-Clarke, *The Occult Roots of Nazism: Secret Aryan Cults and Their Influence on Nazi Ideology* (London: Tauris Parke, rev. edn, 2003).

31 Biggar, *Aiming to Kill*, p. 160.

32 Illora Finlay, 'Ethical Decision-making in Palliative Care: The Clinical Reality', in Paul Badham and Paul Ballard (eds), *Facing Death: An Interdisciplinary Approach* (Cardiff: University of Wales Press, 1996), pp. 64–86, 78.

33 Lord Joffe, cited in Mary Warnock and Elisabeth Macdonald, *Easeful Death: Is There a Case for Assisted Dying?* (Oxford: Oxford University Press, 2008), p. 73.

34 E-mail communication of 21 May 2008.

35 <www.dignityindying.org.uk/information/assisteddying.asp>.

6 Does assisted suicide imply presumption, ingratitude or despair towards God?

1 St Thomas Aquinas, *Summa Theologiae* Question 64, Article 5.

2 W. Blackstone, *Commentaries on the Laws of England*, ed. A. Ryland (London: Sweet, Pheney, Maxwell, Stevens & Sons, 1829), IV, pp. 169–70.

3 I. Kant, *Lectures on Ethics*, cited on <www.philosophy.ed.ac.uk/ug_study/ug_intro/suiquot.pdf>.

4 David Hume, 'On Suicide', *Hume on Religion*, selected and introduced by R. Wollheim, Fontana Library of Theology and Philosophy (London: Collins, 1963), p. 259.

5 Job 7.15–16. In this instance following the updated version of the New English Bible (NEB), namely, the Revised English Bible of 1989 that, in agreement with the Jerusalem Bible, believes that the Hebrew word translated as 'bones' in the RSV should be replaced by the very similar Hebrew word for 'sufferings'. Similar expressions of longing for death appear in Job 3.20–21; 7.3–7; 9.21; 10.1.

6 Job 42.7–16.

7 W. A. Irwin, 'Job', in Matthew Black and H. H. Rowley (eds), *Peake's Commentary on the Bible* (London and Edinburgh: Thomas Nelson and Sons, 1962), pp. 391–408, 391 and 407.

8 Plato, *Phaedo* (Harmondsworth: Penguin, 1962), p. 105.

9 Illora Finlay, 'Ethical Decision-making in Palliative Care: The Clinical Reality', in Paul Badham and Paul Ballard (eds), *Facing Death: An Interdisciplinary Approach* (Cardiff: University of Wales Press, 1996), pp. 64–86, 78.

10 James Boswell, *Life of Johnson* (Routledge, 1859), Vol. 4, p. 148.

11 Luke 15.11–32.

12 Doctrine Commission, *The Mystery of Salvation* (London: Church House Publishing, 1995), p. 199.

13 Pope John Paul II, Encyclical Letter *Redemptor Hominis* (1979), Section 14, para. 3, issued in Rome, 4 March 1979, and available on the Vatican website <http://www.vatican.va/holy_father/john_paul_ii/encyclicals/documents/hf_jp-ii_enc_04031979_redemptor-hominis_en.html>.

14 *Joint Submission from the Church of England House of Bishops and the Roman Catholic Bishops' Conference of England and Wales to the House of Lords Select Committee*, para. 5 <www.cofe.anglican.org/new/newsitem_item2004-10-19-9713099720>.

7 The relevance of the Christian hope to the euthanasia debate

1 Hans Küng and Walter Jens, *A Dignified Dying: A Plea for Personal Responsibility* (London: SCM Press, 1995), p. 39.

2 Küng and Jens, *Dignified Dying*, p. 39.

3 Jeremiah 31.33.

4 2 Corinthians 4.17.

5 Hans Küng, *Eternal Life?* (London: Collins, 1984); Paul Badham, *Christian Beliefs about Life after Death* (London: SPCK, 1978).

6 Frank Morison, *Who Moved the Stone?* (London: Faber, 1930).

7 Tacitus, *Annals* 15/442–446, in J. Stevenson (ed.), *A New Eusebius: Documents Illustrative of the History of the Church to A.D. 337* (London: SPCK, 1963), p. 2; Celsus, in Origen, *Contra Celsum* 2.12 (Oxford: Oxford University Press, 1965), p. 77; *Tractate Sanhedrin* 43b, in C. H. Dodd, *The Founder of Christianity* (London: Collins, 1971), p. 11.

8 Murray Parkes, 'Grief as an Illness', *New Society*, 9 April 1964.

9 Cf. documentation in Chapter 2 of both Badham, *Christian Beliefs about Life after Death* and *Immortality or Extinction?* (London: SPCK, 1984).

10 Carl Gustav Adolf von Harnack, *What Is Christianity?* (1901; London: E. Benn, 5th edn, 1958), pp. 120–1.

11 W. Pannenberg, *Jesus – God and Man* (London: SCM Press, 1970), pp. 63–73; cf. C. F. D. Moule, *The Significance of the Message of the Resurrection of Jesus Christ* (London: SCM Press, 1968), pp. 129–30.

12 A. Chester, 'Eschatology', in G. Jones (ed.), *The Blackwell Companion to Modern Theology* (Oxford: Blackwell, 2004), pp. 244–57, 251, summarizing Moltmann's *Theology of Hope*.

13 Chester, 'Eschatology', p. 256.

14 St Athanasius, *On the Incarnation* (London: Mowbray, 1963), pp. 57–9.

15 Arthur J. Droge and James D. Tabor, *A Noble Death: Suicide and Martyrdom among Jews and Christians in the Ancient World* (San Francisco: Harper SanFrancisco, 1992).

16 J. Neuner and J. Dupuis, *The Christian Faith in the Doctrinal Documents of the Catholic Church* (London: Collins, rev. edn, 1983), p. 691.

17 E.g. by Athenagoras, Tertullian or Irenaeus; cf. the discussion in Badham, *Christian Beliefs about Life after Death*, Chapter 3.

18 2 Corinthians 5.3–4; I take the expression 'inner nature' from the RSV translation of 4.16. The Greek literally means 'the inward of us'.

19 Archbishops' Commission on Christian Doctrine, *Doctrine in the Church of England* (1938; London: SPCK, 1962), p. 209.

20 Doctrine Commission of the Church of England, *The Mystery of Salvation* (London: Church House Publishing, 1995), pp. 10–11.

21 Doctrine Commission of the Church of England, *Mystery of Salvation*, pp. 191–2.

22 Austin Farrer, *Saving Belief* (London: Hodder & Stoughton, 1964), p. 145; John Hick, *Death and Eternal Life* (London: Collins, 1976), pp. 279–95; Badham, *Christian Beliefs about Life after Death*, p. 93.

23 <www.horizon-research.co.uk>.

24 Michael B. Sabom, *Light and Death: One Doctor's Fascinating Account of Near-Death Experiences* (Grand Rapids, Michigan: Zondervan, 1998), p. 41.

25 Susan J. Blackmore, *Dying to Live: Science and the Near-death Experience* (London: Grafton, 1993), pp. 114–15.

26 Penny Sartori, *Near-Death Experiences of Hospitalized Intensive Care Patients: A Five-Year Clinical Study* (Lewiston, NY: Edwin Mellen Press, 2008), pp. 212–15.

27 Antony Flew, 'My Pilgrimage from Atheism to Theism' <www.biola.edu/antonyflew/flew-interview.pdf>, also in print form in *Philosophia Christi*, Winter 2005.

28 Allan Kellehear, *Experiences Near Death: Beyond Medicine and Religion* (Oxford: Oxford University Press, 1996), p. 94.

29 John Hick, *Biology and the Soul* (Cambridge: Cambridge University Press, 1972), p. 25.

30 Richard Swinburne, *Is There a God?* (Oxford: Oxford University Press, 1996), p. 7.

31 Richard Swinburne, *The Evolution of the Soul* (Oxford: Clarendon Press, 1986), pp. 1–2.

32 Keith Ward, *The Battle for the Soul* (London: Hodder & Stoughton, 1985), pp. 149–50.

8 Euthanasia and the problem of suffering

1 Cited from Nigel Biggar, *Aiming to Kill: The Ethics of Suicide and Euthanasia* (London: Darton, Longman & Todd, 2004), p. 50.

2 Hastings Rashdall, *The Idea of Atonement in Christian Theology* (London: Macmillan, 1925), pp. 305, 333, 375, 411.

3 F. D. Maurice, *Theological Essays* (London: Macmillan, 1853), p. 144.

4 Matthew 18.22; Mark 2.27.

5 Luke 15.11–32.

6 Archbishop of Canterbury, 'Assisted Dying for the Terminally Ill Bill', House of Lords, *Hansard*, 12 May 2006, Cols 1196–7.

7 Julia Lawton, *The Dying Process* (London: Routledge, 2000), p. 176.

8 Michael Dunlop Young and Lesley Cullen, *A Good Death: Conversations with East Londoners* (London: Routledge, 1996), p. 134.

9 Tertullian, *Apology* 50.

10 Dietrich Bonhoeffer, *The Cost of Discipleship* (London: SCM Press, 1959).

11 Genesis 3.16.

12 John Keats, *The Letters of John Keats*, ed. Maurice Buxton Forman (London: Oxford University Press, 4th edn, 1952), p. 134.

13 John Hick, *Evil and the God of Love* (London: Macmillan, 1966).

14 BBC News, 9 November 2005: <http://news.bbc.uk/1/hi/health/4418284.stm>.

15 Illora Finlay, 'Ethical Decision-making in Palliative Care: The Clinical Reality', in Paul Badham and Paul Ballard (eds), *Facing Death: An Interdisciplinary Approach* (Cardiff: University of Wales Press, 1996), pp. 64–86, 80.

16 Sherwin Nuland, *How We Die* (London: Chatto & Windus, 1994), p. 263.

17 A. Dickman, 'Pain in Palliative Care: A Review', *The Pharmaceutical Journal*, 2007, pp. 278, 679–82.

18 Jayne Thomas (comp.), *Care of the Dying and the NHS: Some Carers' Views* (London: The Nuffield Trust, 2003).

19 As stated by Baroness Illora Finlay in the Second Reading of the Palliative Care Bill, House of Lords, 23 February 2007.

20 Biggar, *Aiming to Kill*, p. 168.
21 P. Edmonds, S. Karlsen, S. Khan and J. Addington-Hall, 'Comparison of the Palliative Needs of Patients Dying from Chronic Respiratory Diseases and Lung Cancer', *Palliative Care*, 15, 2001, pp. 287–95.
22 Briefing note from Carmen Dupont, Policy and Information Officer, Dignity in Dying, 21 May 2008.
23 Guy Brown, *The Living End: The Future of Death, Aging and Immortality* (Basingstoke: Palgrave Macmillan, 2007).
24 Mary Warnock and Elisabeth Macdonald, *Easeful Death: Is There a Case for Assisted Dying?* (Oxford: Oxford University Press, 2008), p. 111.
25 Illora Finlay, 'Ethical Decision-making in Palliative Care: The Clinical Reality', in Paul Badham and Paul Ballard (eds), *Facing Death: An Interdisciplinary Approach* (Cardiff: University of Wales Press, 1996), pp. 64–86, 69.
26 Finlay, 'Ethical Decision-making in Palliative Care', p. 72.
27 Julia Lawton, *The Dying Process* (London: Routledge, 2000), p. 19.
28 Julian Anthony Walter, *The Revival of Death* (London: Routledge, 1994), p. 167.
29 Brown, *Living End*, p. 79.
30 Lawton, *Dying Process*, p. vii.
31 Lawton, *Dying Process*, p. 181.
32 Lawton, *Dying Process*, p. vii.
33 Lawton, *Dying Process*, p. 182.
34 Lawton, *Dying Process*, p. 131.
35 Lawton, *Dying Process*, p. 179.
36 Lawton, *Dying Process*, p. 182.
37 BBC News, 27 April 2008, <http://news.bbc.co.uk/1/hi/health/7363525.stm>.
38 Office of Disease Prevention and Epidemiology, Oregon Department of Human Services, *Seventh Annual Report on Oregon's Death with Dignity Act* (2005), p. 24.
39 John Keown, *Considering Physician-Assisted Suicide: An Evaluation of Lord Joffe's Assisted Dying for the Terminally Ill Bill* (London: Care Not Killing Alliance, 2006), p. 15.
40 Young and Cullen, *Good Death*, p. 136.
41 Patrick Nowell Smith, 'The Right to Die', in Paul Badham (ed.), *Ethics on the Frontiers of Human Existence* (New York: Paragon House, 1992), pp. 209–22.
42 Hans Küng and Walter Jens, *A Dignified Dying: A Plea for Personal Responsibility* (London: SCM Press, 1995), pp. 34, 38, 119–21.

9 End-of-life decision-making in the Netherlands, Oregon and Britain

1 Mary Warnock and Elisabeth Macdonald, *Easeful Death: Is There a Case for Assisted Dying?* (Oxford: Oxford University Press, 2008), p. x.

2 John Keown, *Considering Physician-Assisted Suicide: An Evaluation of Lord Joffe's Assisted Dying for the Terminally Ill Bill* (London: Care Not Killing Alliance, 2006), pp. 4–5.

3 Marvin Newman, 'Voluntary Active Euthanasia', in Paul Badham and others, *Perspectives on Death and Dying* (Philadelphia, Pennsylvania: The Charles Press, 1989), pp. 173–87, 179.

4 Nigel Biggar, *Aiming to Kill: The Ethics of Suicide and Euthanasia* (London: Darton, Longman & Todd, 2004), p. 126.

5 Mary Warnock and Elisabeth Macdonald, *Easeful Death: Is There a Case for Assisted Dying?* (Oxford: Oxford University Press, 2008), pp. 28–33; and cf. Ruurd Veldhuis, 'Tired of Living, Afraid of Dying: Reflections on the Practice of Euthanasia in The Netherlands', *Studies in Christian Ethics*, 11.1, 1998, pp. 63–76, 74.

6 Penney Lewis, *Assisted Dying and Legal Change* (Oxford: Oxford University Press, 2007), p. 96, note 120.

7 Biggar, *Aiming to Kill*, p. 251.

8 Illora Finlay, 'Ethical Decision-making in Palliative Care: The Clinical Reality', in Paul Badham and Paul Ballard (eds), *Facing Death: An Interdisciplinary Approach* (Cardiff: University of Wales Press, 1996), pp. 64–86, 82.

9 Biggar, *Aiming to Kill*, p. 129.

10 John Keown, *Considering Physician-Assisted Suicide: An Evaluation of Lord Joffe's Assisted Dying for the Terminally Ill Bill* (London: Care Not Killing Alliance, 2006), p. 8.

11 Lewis, *Assisted Dying and Legal Change*.

12 Margaret Otlowski, *Voluntary Euthanasia and the Common Law* (Oxford: Clarendon Press, 1997), p. 437.

13 Warnock and Macdonald, *Easeful Death*, p. 84.

14 Keown, *Considering Physician-Assisted Suicide*, p. 6.

15 Veldhuis, 'Tired of Living, Afraid of Dying', p. 69.

16 Lewis, *Assisted Dying and Legal Change*, pp. 170–6, note 59.

17 Cited in Brown, *Living End*, p. 84.

18 Johannes J. M. van Delden, 'The Remmelink Study Two Years Later', p. 27, cited by Lewis, *Assisted Dying and Legal Change*, p. 187.

19 Clive Seale, 'National Survey of End-of-life Decisions Made by UK Medical Practitioners', *Palliative Medicine*, 20, 2006, pp. 3–10.
20 John Griffiths, 'Comparative Reflections: Is the Dutch Case Unique?', in Albert Klijn et al. (eds), *Regulating Physician-Negotiated Death* (Amsterdam: Elsevier, 2001), pp. 9 and 201, in Lewis, *Assisted Dying and Legal Change*, p. 185.
21 Helga Kuhse, 'From Intention to Consent Learning from Experience with Euthanasia', p. 67, cited in Lewis, *Assisted Dying and Legal Change*, p. 183.
22 Clive Seale, 'Characteristics of End-of-life Decisions: Survey of UK Medical Practitioners', *Palliative Medicine*, 20, 2006, pp. 653–9.
23 Agnes van der Heide, and others, 'End-of-life Decision-making in Six European Countries', *The Lancet*, 362, 2003, pp. 343–50.
24 Helge Kuhse, 'End-of-life Decisions in Australian Medial Practice', cited in Lewis, *Assisted Dying and Legal Change*, p. 183.
25 YouGov poll 2004, in Dignity in Dying, *The Report* (London: Dignity in Dying, 2006), p. 19.
26 Dignity in Dying, *The Report* (London: Dignity in Dying, 2006), p. 19, citing a report by Z. Kmietovicz, 'R.E.S.P.E.C.T – why doctors are still getting enough of it', *British Medical Journal*, 2002; 324 (7328).
27 H. Kuhse and P. Singer, 'Editorial', *Bioethics*, 3, 1992, p. 4, cited in Otlowski, *Voluntary Euthanasia and the Common Law*, p. 439.
28 Warnock and Macdonald, *Easeful Death*, p. 85.
29 Biggar, *Aiming to Kill*, p. 151.
30 Otlowski, *Voluntary Euthanasia and the Common Law*, p. 437.
31 Lewis, *Assisted Dying and Legal Change*, p. 186.
32 Kuhse, 'End-of-life Decisions in Australian Medical Practice', p. 176.
33 Cited in Warnock and Macdonald, *Easeful Death*, p. 119.
34 Luc Deliens, 'End-of-life Decisions in Flanders, Belgium', cited in Lewis, *Assisted Dying and Legal Change*, p. 176.
35 Margaret Battin, Agnes van der Heide, Linda Ganzini, Gerrit van der Wal and Brejie D. Onwuteaka-Philipsen, 'Legal Physician-assisted Dying in Oregon and The Netherlands: Evidence concerning the Impact on Patients in "Vulnerable Groups"', *Journal of Medical Ethics*, 33, 2007, p. 592.
36 Battin and others, 'Legal Physician-assisted Dying in Oregon and The Netherlands', p. 597.
37 Raymond Tallis, A Doctor's Dilemma, House of Lords Committee, 19 April 2006, p. 7.

38 Ann Jackson, The Reality of Assisted Dying in Oregon: 'Draft Notes of Compassion in Dying: All Party Parliamentary Group Meeting', House of Lords Committee Room 4b, 19 April 2006, p. 11.

39 Jackson, Reality of Assisted Dying in Oregon, p. 11.

40 Tallis, Doctor's Dilemma, p. 6.

41 Jackson, Reality of Assisted Dying in Oregon, p. 2.

42 Jackson, Reality of Assisted Dying in Oregon, p. 3.

43 <http://oregon.gov/DHS/ph/pas/index.shtml>.

44 Jackson, Reality of Assisted Dying in Oregon, p. 3.

45 Otlowski, *Voluntary Euthanasia and the Common Law*, p. 441.

46 Veldhuis, 'Tired of Living, Afraid of Dying'.

10 A Christian case for assisted dying

1 As E. C. Moore said of Ritschl's analysis of Christian pietism in his *Christian Thought since Kant* (London: Duckworth, 1912), p. 98.

2 Nigel Biggar, *Aiming to Kill: The Ethics of Suicide and Euthanasia* (London: Darton, Longman & Todd, 2004), pp. iv and v.

3 Stephen Williams, 'The Case against Euthanasia', in Paul Badham and Paul Ballard (eds), *Facing Death: An Interdisciplinary Approach* (Cardiff: University of Wales Press, 1996), pp. 117–29, 118–19, 123–4.

4 R. M. Hare, *Essays on Bioethics* (Oxford: Clarendon Press, 1993), p. 72, cited by Williams, 'Case against Euthanasia', p. 127.

5 <www.dignityindying.org.uk>.

6 Luke 15.11–32.

7 Basil Hume, *To Be a Pilgrim: A Spiritual Notebook* (London: SPCK, 1984), p. 226.

8 *Sunday Times*, 7 September 1997.

9 <www.sacred-heart.org.uk/newsletter-2006-13.html>.

10 Dietrich Bonhoeffer, *Letters and Papers from Prison*, Fontana Books (London: Collins, 1963), p. 11.

11 Bonhoeffer, *Letters and Papers from Prison*, p. 163.

12 Bonhoeffer, *Letters and Papers from Prison*, pp. 74–5.

13 St Athanasius, *On the Incarnation* (London: Mowbray, 1963), pp. 57–9.

14 Julia Lawton, *The Dying Process* (London: Routledge, 2007), pp. 176, 132, 95.

15 Mary Warnock and Elisabeth Macdonald, *Easeful Death: Is There a Case for Assisted Dying?* (Oxford: Oxford University Press, 2008), p. 137.

16 Warnock and Macdonald, *Easeful Death*, p. 111.

17 Lawton, *Dying Process*, pp. 120–1.
18 Ruurd Veldhuis, 'Tired of Living, Afraid of Dying: Reflections on the Practice of Euthanasia in The Netherlands', *Studies in Christian Ethics*, 11.1, 1998, pp. 63–76, 70.
19 Warnock and Macdonald, *Easeful Death*, p. xi.
20 In Plato's *Phaedo*. This is collected with some other writings and marketed as Plato, *The Last Days of Socrates* (Harmondsworth: Penguin, 1967).
21 'O strength and stay upholding all creation'.

Select bibliography

Badham, Paul (2005), 'MCU Submission on the Assisted Dying Bill', *Modern Believing* 46.1 (April), pp. 46–51.

Badham, Paul (ed.) (1992), *Ethics on the Frontiers of Human Existence*, New York: Paragon House.

Badham, Paul, and others (1989), *Perspectives on Death and Dying*, Philadelphia, Pennsylvania: The Charles Press.

Badham, Paul, and Paul Ballard (eds) (1996), *Facing Death: An Interdisciplinary Approach*, Cardiff: University of Wales Press.

Biggar, Nigel (2004), *Aiming to Kill: The Ethics of Suicide and Euthanasia*, London: Darton, Longman & Todd.

Brown, Guy (2007), *The Living End: The Future of Death, Aging and Immortality*, Basingstoke: Palgrave Macmillan.

Dignity in Dying (2006), *The Report*, London: Dignity in Dying.

Fletcher, Joseph (1966), *Situation Ethics: The New Morality*, London: SCM Press.

Gill, Robin (ed.) (1998), *Euthanasia and the Churches*, London: Cassell.

House of Lords (1994), *Report of the Select Committee on Medical Ethics*, London: HMSO, 31 January.

Keown, John (2006), *Considering Physician-Assisted Suicide: An Evaluation of Lord Joffe's Assisted Dying for the Terminally Ill Bill*, London: Care Not Killing Alliance.

Küng, Hans, and Walter Jens (1995), *A Dignified Dying: A Plea for Personal Responsibility*, London: SCM Press.

Lawton, Julia (2000), *The Dying Process: Patients' Experience of Palliative Care*, London: Routledge.

Lewis, Penney (2007), *Assisted Dying and Legal Change*, Oxford: Oxford University Press.

Otlowski, Margaret (1997), *Voluntary Euthanasia and the Common Law*, Oxford: Clarendon Press.

Seale, Clive (2006a), 'Characteristics of End-of-Life Decisions: Survey of UK Medical Practitioners', *Palliative Medicine*, pp. 653–9.

Seale, Clive (2006b), 'National Survey of End-of-Life Decisions Made by UK Medical Practitioners', *Palliative Medicine*, pp. 3–10.

Veldhuis, Ruurd (1998), 'Tired of Living, Afraid of Dying: Reflections on the Practice of Euthanasia in The Netherlands', *Studies in Christian Ethics*, 11.1, pp. 63–76.

Select bibliography

Warnock, Mary, and Elisabeth Macdonald (2008), *Easeful Death: Is There a Case for Assisted Dying?*, Oxford: Oxford University Press.

Young, Michael Dunlop, and Lesley Cullen (1996), *A Good Death: Conversations with East Londoners*, London: Routledge.

Index

Index

Index